My Andrew

My Andrew

Day-to-Day Living with a Child with an Autism Spectrum Disorder

Wallis A. Simpson

Autism Asperger Publishing Co.
P.O. Box 23173
Shawnee Mission, Kansas 66283-0173
www.asperger.net

© 2007 Autism Asperger Publishing Co.
P.O. Box 23173
Shawnee Mission, Kansas 66283-0173
www.asperger.net

Formerly published under the insignia of iUniverse, Inc. (0-595-33113-0)

Publisher's Cataloging-in-Publication

Simpson, Wallis A.

My Andrew : day-to-day living with a child with an autism spectrum disorder / Wallis A. Simpson. -- 1st ed. -- Shawnee Mission, KS : Autism Asperger Pub. Co., 2007.

p. ; cm.

ISBN-13: 978-1-931282-30-7
ISBN-10: 1-931282-30-7
LCCN: 2006932220
Includes bibliographical references.

1. Autism in children. 2. Autistic children--Care. 3. Autistic children--Family relationships. 4. Parents of autistic children--Family relationships. 5. Simpson, Andrew. 6. Simpson, Wallis A. I. Title.

RJ506.A9 S56 2006
618.92/85882--dc22   0610

Printed in Palatino.

Printed in the United States of America.

Contents

Preface

Discovering that your child has a permanent, pervasive disorder is a shock to any parent. At first, you cannot believe that the diagnosis is true. But quickly, you begin to immerse yourself in information to learn as much as you can, as quickly as you can. You read every book you can get your hands on that you think might help you on the road you now must travel. It was that way for my husband and me when our son Andrew was diagnosed with ASD or autism spectrum disorder.

Having a child with special needs is an emotional roller-coaster ride of love, joy, pride, frustration, anger, and deep sadness. Most often, the love and sadness win. Every little victory is celebrated. Every setback hurts. There are not enough books on the shelves to prepare a family for getting up and living each day with these special children.

According to the Autism Society of America, autism is a complex developmental disability that typically appears during the first three years of life. It is a neurological disorder that impacts the development of the brain in the areas of social interaction and communication skills. It is four times more prevalent in boys than in girls.

Autism is one of five disorders coming under the umbrella of Pervasive Developmental Disorders (PDD). This umbrella also known as ASD includes Autistic Disorder, Asperger's Disorder, Childhood Disintegrative Disorder (CDD), Rhett's Disorder, and PDD-Not Otherwise Specified (PDD-NOS). For more information, visit the website of the Autism Society of America at www.autism-society.org.

Because autism is a spectrum disorder, the symptoms and characteristics can present themselves in a wide variety of combination, from mild to severe. Children and adults with ASD can exhibit any combination of behaviors in any degree of severity. It is a very individualized disorder, which makes it one of mystery and loneliness. No other child has the same combination of symptoms to the same level of intensity. Therefore, while you can relate to others, no one goes through the exact same experiences. Because it is a pervasive disorder, there is no aspect of the child that is not affected. It "pervades" or permeates all developmental areas.

I was once asked what I felt was the most difficult thing about autism. My answer is that it is the uncertainty of the day-to-day living with an autistic child. To illustrate, let's look at something as apparently simple as communication. There are four parts to the communication model. Part one, you take in information. Part two, you relate this information to something you already know. Part three, you formulate an appropriate response. Part four, you give the appropriate response. For most people, these steps happen without any conscious thought. If a person has a learning disability, there is often a breakdown in one of the four parts that must be compensated for. But for the child with autism, the breakdown can occur in any one of the four parts, at any time, on any given day.

There are days when Andrew knows what we want, but he struggles to give the appropriate response. Some days, Andrew cannot seem to process the information in the first place. What he could do yesterday, he cannot do today. Tomorrow, he may appear perfectly normal with all four parts of the communication model working smoothly. But those days are extremely rare. The breakdowns cause great frustration because every day when we wake up, we have to figure out where the breakdown may be occurring for today and make the necessary adjustments to our expectations.

The key to Andrew's progress thus far has been early intervention. I truly believe that any effort made during the first five or six years of a child's life are worth it for the payoffs that are seen in the later years. Gathering a support group of loving and caring people is essential. Family, friends, and professionals are all part of the team necessary to help each child reach his or her full potential, while also providing the support parents or caregivers need.

I have come to learn that it is okay to cry, to be angry, to hurt, to rejoice over the little things, and to fully embrace all the things about my son that make him so very precious to us. We have what we call "survival days": those days when you know nothing you do or say will be right. Those are the days when you let go of any expectations and hang on until bedtime, knowing tomorrow is bound to be better. And so far, tomorrow has almost always been better. I tell Andrew all the time that he is my sweet boy and he always will be. Love truly conquers all.

One of my best stress releasers has been to write. In compiling a chronological journal of our day-to-day living with Andrew, we have been able to see the progress Andrew has made and the journey we've taken to get him this far. It is my hope and prayer that in sharing our journey, we may help someone else to feel a little less alone in theirs.

– Wallis A. Simpson

Welcome Andrew:
When Everything Was Normal

❖

(September 1996 – September 1998)

September 27, 1996

Dear Andrew, You're finally here! How I've waited for this day. My
8 pound, 4 ounce bundle of joy. You took your sweet time – a week
late! But you're here now. All the difficulties, all the scares of the past
seven months are over and are now worth it. I love your dark hair,
your long fingers, and the cooing sound you make. You feel so good in
my arms. Everyone is anxious to see you.

You have a big brother, Jesse, who is two and a half. He is ready to
play and teach you many things. You also have Grandma and Grand-
pa, Mema and Geda (Donald's parents), and several aunts, uncles,
and cousins. None of them lives close by but we will see them often.
I'm so glad you are here. Welcome, my sweet Andrew, my sweet boy.
Mommy loves you.

October 9, 1996

Andrew is pretty wonderful. He has usually one crying spell each
evening when he has bubbles. His night schedule is very reasonable.
At his two-week check-up, he weighed 9 lbs., 2 oz. and was 21 inches
long. Everything is normal.

December 4, 1996

Today at his two-month check-up, Andrew already weighs 13 lbs., 9.3
oz. and is 24 inches long. He is sleeping up to six hours at a time. I'm
so glad. Between taking care of him, Jesse, and our new puppy, I'm
exhausted. The pediatrician says we need to work on his back strength

1

and lifting his head from a prone position. Jesse is doing better having Andrew around. He was excited for a few days, but then he started calling him "that baby." Lately, he has changed it to "my Andrew." He's been sweet. I look forward to seeing them grow closer as brothers.

Christmas 1996

Andrew is three months old. He loves to laugh and be tickled. He is becoming very social: smiles spontaneously, tries to giggle, "talks" in conversation. He likes to be held and burped, facing away from the person holding him. He won't take his bottle if he has a burp. He is my sweet boy.

January 29, 1997

Andrew has been sick for three days: fever, coughing occasionally, nose congested, and his ears are infected.

March 13, 1997

He has had fever off and on again for three days, and his ears have been infected for over a week. He also has a viral rash on his face. The ear infections have not responded to Amoxicillin so they are putting him on Ceclor. He has the best belly laugh I've ever heard. He thinks his Daddy is very funny.

April 24, 1997

It's only been a month, and Andrew's ears are infected again. What is going on? He's on Ceclor again and his tummy hurts from nasal discharge. On top of that, he is teething.

May 6, 1997

The doctor followed up on Andrew's ear infection. His ear drum has a dull color but there is no pus. The pediatrician wants to continue the Ceclor. I'm getting concerned about all these antibiotics. On the bright side, Andrew likes to play hide-and-seek with his blanket and gets excited when he sees Pooh Bear or the Pooh on his curtains. He is standing up and just needs to move his feet to be mobile.

July 11, 1997

The pediatrician is concerned about Andrew's ear infections. So, she referred us to an ENT doctor (Ear-Nose-Throat). We've seen him twice in the past two weeks. Andrew's been on Augmentin for eleven days. The infections have cleared up, but the doctor is considering putting him on more antibiotics next winter as a precautionary measure.

August 15, 1997

I took Andrew to the doctor last week. He was clawing at his ears and waking up at night crying. Overall, he's been miserable. The doctor thought he was irritable from teething. She mentioned doing some sleep training by pushing his bedtime back a little. Last night, he woke up with fever. I took Andrew to the pediatrician this morning and, sure enough, his ears are infected again. He is taking more Augmentin this time. Poor little guy. I wish we could keep him well.

August 27, 1997

Twelve days later and the infection is still not cleared up. We've switched to Amoxicillin and will keep him on it for the next three to six months.

[Author's note: I have not found any scientific data to back the claim that children with ASD have a higher rate of chronic ear infections than other children. However, an informal study over the years of asking numerous other parents finds that chronic ear infections do seem to be prevalent among children with ASD. Parents and doctors often feel the ear infections are the cause of speech delays, which can mask the autistic symptom of lack of or delayed communication skills.]

September 20, 1997

One week short of his first birthday and Andrew has taken his first steps. He is such a doll! I can't get over what a beautiful boy he is … and I'm not saying that just because he looks like I did at that age! His whole face lights up when he smiles. He makes me smile all the time.

September 27, 1997

Happy Birthday, Andrew! Are you already a year old? It doesn't seem possible. You are growing so big. The doctor said you weigh just over 23 pounds. I love your smile and your belly laugh. I can't wait for you to start talking. I know you understand us. And Jesse is so anxious to teach you all the things big brothers are supposed to. You are my sweet boy. You always will be.

Christmas 1997

Andrew is fifteen months old. His favorite toy is a beeper, and his favorite gift is the bows on the packages. He is learning to nod "yes." It's about time.

January 9, 1998

Andrew is so cute but he still doesn't talk. He doesn't say any real words. I'm beginning to wonder if that's my fault. I wonder if it is because I don't work with him enough that he isn't saying any words. Plus, I still haven't weaned him off the bottle. He enjoys it and I love to hold him. It's hard to know if this is normal or not. Jesse did everything so much earlier than "normal." I guess we'll just wait and see.

January 12, 1998

He had a barky cough last night after having a lesser cough over the weekend. Now he is running a fever and the doctor found fluid behind his ears. We have to continue giving him the Amoxicillin. It is so frustrating. If he is constantly taking the antibiotics, why is he still having problems with his ears? I know he is miserable. That makes us miserable, too.

February 1998

At seventeen months, Andrew loves to kick the football and tackle Daddy. He is fascinated with the rotor blades on his toy helicopter. He watches his favorite video, *Green Eggs and Ham*, over and over. I can't decide if he will be right- or left-handed. He reaches with his left hand but eats and plays with either hand. He likes to cover his head and walk around the house, and he loves to dance.

March 23, 1998

We've been concerned about Andrew's lack of speech. Sometimes it seems as if he doesn't hear us very well, so we took him to have his hearing tested. They did not find any apparent hearing problems. I'm glad, but it doesn't tell us why he doesn't seem to hear us.

[Author's note: Delayed speech is a common, early symptom of ASD. Many parents express concern about an apparent hearing loss and have their child tested. Children with ASD turn their attention inward in an attempt to tune out overwhelming stimuli in the environment. It is important to note that these children usually have hypersensitivity to one or more environmental stimuli: sights, sounds, smells, temperature, pain, or touch.]

April 3, 1998

Andrew's eyes are red and puffy and his eyelids have been matting for two days. Now he has conjunctivitis on top of everything else.

April 27, 1998

Andrew is nineteen months. He loves to play with his little tool bench. He is still eating with either his left or right hand so I'm still not sure which hand will be his dominant one. He does color with his right hand though. He is finally saying a few words: Momma, Grr Momma (for Grandma), kitty, hooray, and "yes." It's a start.

July 8, 1998

Andrew was pulling at his ear last night in addition to having a fever and diarrhea. The pediatrician found a severe infection in his left ear today when I took him in and an early infection in the right. Augmentin was prescribed again. I wouldn't be surprised if the doctor's office names one of their rooms after us some day. We sure seem to be there a lot.

July 20, 1998

We had Andrew's ears rechecked. They are much better. The pediatrician says that all the re-occurring infections have caused the speech delay. We are being referred back to the ENT doctor for ear tubes. It's such a scary thought. We almost had to have tubes put in Jesse's ears, but he suddenly stopped having infections. Perhaps the same thing will happen with Andrew. He's such a little guy to be undergoing surgery even though it is considered minor.

July 28, 1998

Andrew tries to talk all the time now and we can actually understand some of it. It is such a relief, even if he does get some things mixed up. For example, he calls both Donald and me "Mommy." That drives Donald nuts. He will say "no" for both "yes" and "no." He loves to do the wooden number puzzle and can kick the soccer ball really well.

August 10, 1998

We were at the ENT to get a hearing test. Andrew cried because he was scared of the toys. As a result, they couldn't complete the test, but they did enough to conclude that they think his hearing is okay. The operation to place the tubes in his ears is set for the 14th – this Friday. I can't believe we're really going to let them do this. I know it is a common procedure but that's my little boy they are talking about. He's not even two. I hope he does okay. I hope I'm okay, too. I really do.

August 14, 1998

The surgery went well. There were no complications. It was harder on me than I ever dreamed possible. Donald stayed home with Jesse and I took Andrew to the hospital at 5:30 a.m. They gave him something to put him to sleep, but he wasn't asleep when they took him from my arms. That was even harder than trying to calm him when he woke up. I had to go to the doctor's lounge and cry for five minutes before I could make my way to the waiting room. Suddenly, my big boy seemed so little. This surgery had better work.

September 27, 1998

Another happy birthday, Andrew! Two years old today. I would say we are entering the "terrible twos" except I think you entered them several months ago. Still, it is wonderful to see you growing and learning, and to watch your personality developing. It's funny the way you refuse to play Jesse's games by Jesse's rules. Your brother can be so bossy but it doesn't seem to bother you at all. You can be so stubborn. I wonder what this next year will bring. Hopefully, you won't have any more ear infections so you can start talking with us. I'm sure you will catch up quickly. You seem to have a lot to tell us. Happy birthday, sweet boy.

The Terrible Twos:
A Forewarning of Things to Come

❖

(October 1998 – September 1999)

October 9, 1998

We had our two-year check-up today. Actually, it was more because Andrew has been teething and in a lot of pain. Sometimes he plays with his ears, which worries me. He has also been waking up in the middle of the night with nightmares. They are scary. He still doesn't communicate with us well, so often I don't know what has scared him or how to calm him down. Any way, Andrew threw one of his classic temper tantrums right in the doctor's office. It's the kind where he yells at everyone, hits and claws at me, and then throws himself on the floor, thrashing around. It was so embarrassing. I know that two-year-olds are supposed to be defiant and oppositional. They are known for their temper tantrums. But something doesn't seem right. I can't place my finger on it, but it just seems different.

The doctor talked with me for about fifteen minutes. She feels Andrew's frustration is from his lack of the ability to communicate. She gave me a few suggestions for handling the hitting and tantrums. She also gave some suggestions for helping him communicate. Maybe they will work.

He has added three more words: "O-tay" [okay], "Aw Rit" [alright], and "No Way!" He shares a room and bunk beds with Jesse but he prefers to sleep on the floor. His favorite things to do are watching *Veggie Tales* movies and play with Murphy, our dog.

[Author's note: Most neurotypical ("normal") children show a few symptoms of ASD. The difference in children with ASD is the number and severity of symptoms as well as the inappropriateness of the behaviors for the child's age.]

7

November 13, 1998

Andrew spent all night getting sick every hour. He woke up with a barky cough, wheezing, and unable to catch his breath. The doctor says he has the croup so I did a steam shower and then took him outside in the cold. I've never had to do that before.

December 7, 1998

Andrew had a low-grade fever yesterday afternoon and evening. This morning, he had crusty, bloody discharge from his ear. Another ear infection. This is so frustrating! I thought the tubes were supposed to keep him from having them any more. What is it going to take to get him well?

Christmas 1998

Andrew is two years, three months old. He likes his *ABC Song & Book* and will sit to be read to but turns the pages really fast. He pretends to write the ABCs. His favorite Christmas toys are the play camera, Larry Boy pencil, Elmo computer game, and a telephone.

January 25, 1999

We went back to the ENT, who tried to get a hearing test. Andrew was scared of the toy puppy that barks, but he could respond to lights in the booth. Everything seems okay. At least the ear infections haven't damaged his ability to hear. Both tubes are beginning to loosen. Andrew is growing so fast that he may lose the tubes soon. Then where will we be?

March 3, 1999

Andrew has developed quite a temper these days. He hits and screams at the drop of a hat. We have found that time-out in his room works wonders. He hates that and is ready to cooperate immediately whenever he is being escorted to his room.

He is talking more and more every day and is starting to use incomplete sentences: "Jesse school"; "Daddy work"; and my favorite, "Jesse, calm down!" He won't leave the TV buttons alone. If the TV is on, he turns it off, changes the channel, or turns the volume up. If it's off, he turns it on. No matter how many times I slap his hand or remove him from the room or turn whatever he's watching off, he just goes right back to it. He is a stubborn kid.

April 12, 1999

Andrew is running a low-grade fever and has had earaches off and on for the past few days. He is mildly congested, but his ears are not infected. The doctor didn't see either ear tube. Could he have lost them already? He weighs 32 lbs. and is 38 inches tall. He is taller than Jesse was at this age.

May 12, 1999

Last night around 11:15, Andrew started screaming. I couldn't make him stop crying and yelling, and I was so frustrated. The only way Donald could get him to stop was to hold him real tight and then lightly shake him. He got him to wake up enough to be comforted. Within two minutes, Andrew was on his bed, quiet and going back to sleep. He can be such a handful. He is addicted to *CNN Headline News*. He is constantly climbing things like the chain link fence or the lattice arbor. He is a whirlwind.

July 11, 1999

Like a typical two-year-old, Andrew isn't thrilled with consequences. His favorite word is, of course, "no." This morning, he got in trouble five times before he finally did what he was supposed to. As soon as he decided he would obey, he quit crying and was fine. He is such a stubborn kid.

July 28, 1999

We videotaped Andrew "singing" with the toddler class for Vacation Bible School Family Night. It was a riot, and he was a big success with his antics. At one point, he actually tried to sing a little.

He is watching a movie in Winnie-the-Pooh underwear (sitting on a towel). He is so close to potty training but he loves his diapers. I was doing some sorting of Jesse's clothes when he saw the underwear. I asked Andrew if he wanted to wear them and he said yes. I'm just waiting for the accident but it's a start. He has gotten up in the morning a few times completely dry, and he hides in the corner of the room when he is having a bowel movement. I'm trying not to push but it sure will be nice to be out of the diapers!

[Author's note: Some children with ASD have difficulty with toilet training issues. We were fortunate that Andrew did not have any delays in this area.]

August 27, 1999

Andrew and Jesse have been fighting like cats and dogs lately. When Jesse starts school Monday, it will be good to have some one-on-one time with Andrew. I know he's pretty typical for a soon-to-be three-year-old, but his speech bothers me. It's not very clear. His attention span is almost non-existent. It will be good for him to do things without Jesse's constant presence. Plus it will be good for Jesse to have some time away from Andrew.

September 23, 1999

Andrew has finally gotten the idea that his birthday is coming. I'm sure he doesn't have a clue what that really means but he has equated it with getting presents. Now he walks around saying, "Haddy Birday to!" His favorite movie and book right now is "Sno Wipe" (*Snow White*). He walks into church marching and trying to sing *Hi Ho*. It's funny.

I had heard that our school district is offering free screening for kids with possible speech/language problems. A nursery worker at church has encouraged us to get Andrew tested. I guess it wouldn't hurt. It will have to wait a little while. I understand they've had nearly eighty children to test so we'll wait our turn. We're not in any hurry. Andrew's a happy kid even if you don't know what he's saying half the time.

September 27, 1999

Happy birthday, Andrew. We made it through the twos. I'm so glad. It's been a rough year but I know it will get better. I love watching you kick the ball and wrestle with Daddy. Yes, you and Jesse don't get along the best but that's just because you won't do what he tells you to. Any day now, you could break out into full sentences and then maybe you won't be so frustrated. It's going to be a great year. I just know it. I love you, sweet boy. And you are my sweet boy. You always will be.

Our World Is Changing: Developmentally Delayed

❖

(October 1999 – September 2000)

October 3, 1999

We had Andrew participate in the free screening by the school district on Friday for speech and language development. We hadn't been there for ten minutes before the lady and her assistant were recommending a full screening for him. There are some other concerns, too, like his social development. The screener pegged him on some of her questions, like his fixation on certain foods and toys and his high threshold of pain. She mentioned some disorder that has some symptoms of autism. Andrew is *not* autistic, but apparently there is some kind of disorder where a child can be high functioning, have high intelligence and still have these tendencies that delay speech/language and social development. I don't have a lot of details, but it made some sense to me.

When I told him, Donald was depressed about it at first but then he was better. We know Andrew isn't autistic, but it's nice to know that there may be a legitimate, physical reason for some of his behavior. It will be good to get the evaluation done so we can figure out how we can best help him. I do love my baby.

[Author's note: Even with a psychology degree, I did not recognize that the symptoms in Andrew were autistic in nature. I was also a mother in denial. I have found that most people have only had exposure to autism through the movie *Rain Man*: the story of a profoundly affected autistic man. If that is the only exposure one has had, it is easy to see why a diagnosis of autism might bring denial and fear. Doctors and researchers are learning more about ASD every day. While there is

11

no known cause or cure, help and support have grown tremendously in previous decades. There is now more reason to be hopeful for meaningful answers than ever before.]

October 12, 1999

Andrew is pretty much the same. I never really noticed his fixation on certain foods and toys. I just thought he was a picky eater. It never bothered me before. Now I think about it often. I'm supposed to take him to the doctor in a few weeks. I think I'll ask her about it. Andrew has taken an interest in a puzzle of the United States. He even knows where some of the states go. He has also been doing more coloring lately.

October 22, 1999

Today was our doctor's visit. Andrew is 40 inches tall. I mentioned my concerns to the doctor: how he often wakes at night searching for a lost toy; how he eats regular foods but is very picky; and how he often refuses to respond to our verbal questions. He only answers yes or no questions but can use some sentences. He has fairly clear speech but not a lot of vocabulary. He plays jokes, teases, and smiles, but does not tolerate handling or touch by strangers. Also, he has spells at the table or other brief periods of staring, totally "out of it," but then seems fine. Because of his staring spells, the doctor is referring us to the hospital for EEG testing. This is becoming a nightmare.

[Author's note: An EEG or electroencephalogram is a record of brain activity that can help diagnosis seizure disorders like epilepsy, some kinds of infections, metabolic disturbances, and sleep disorders. For more information, visit www.kidshealth.org/parent/system/medical/eeg.html]

November 9, 1999

Andrew's full screening by the school district went very well today. He was in a good mood, so he cooperated. Donald and I will meet with their team next Tuesday afternoon for the formal follow-up. We already know he will qualify for at least one of their programs, a preschool class that meets twice a week. The therapist could tell us that much.

November 16, 1999

We had the meeting for the results of Andrew's testing this afternoon.

We are encouraged, although I confess to a level of frustration, too. We met with a six-member team from the school for over an hour and a half. Basically, Andrew qualifies for their special education preschool program in all four areas tested: gross-motor skills, fine-motor skills, social skills, and speech. Their biggest concern is his language development. Right now, he communicates at the level of a two-year, two-month-old. In one area, it's as low as one year, eleven months. He has very little language of his own. It's almost all echolalia speech: words, phrases, or sentences he has memorized from hearing them repeatedly. They will also work with him on articulation, and some fine gross-motor skills, and large gross-motor skills. He has what they are calling splintered development. In a few areas, he is advanced for his age. In most areas, he is behind.

They are recommending he start the program the week after Thanksgiving. It is two full days a week. There are five other kids in the class. We have set up an IEP (Individualized Education Program). The teacher and three therapists who will work with Andrew have each set goals that they will work on with him over the next year. It's encouraging to know that they feel they can help Andrew over the next three years before he starts kindergarten. We have heard positive things about this program from several sources. Thursday I am going to sit in on the class to observe for a while. It's a little frustrating to realize just how developmentally delayed Andrew really is. Donald and I are both very glad, though, that we have help now. This will be good for him.

[Author's note: The Individuals with Disabilities Education Act (IDEA) is a law that ensures that all children with disabilities receive a free, appropriate public education in the least restrictive environment. An IEP is an education plan tailor-made for a child's individual needs. A team consisting of teachers, therapists, administrators, and the parents outline the educational goals, objectives, and evaluation standards for the child. This plan is usually updated yearly. For more information, visit www.ed.gov/parents/needs/speced/iepguide]

November 22, 1999

I've struggled this week to adjust to Andrew's limitations. I know I need to work on my expectations. I have been and I will continue to. He's my baby and a sweetheart. His bear hugs and kisses warm my heart. God will take care of him.

Christmas 1999

Andrew is three years, three months old. In many ways, he is still two. He only has two volumes: loud and louder. He is constantly chattering, even when alone. The trouble is, only a few words are understandable. He was sick Christmas Eve.

He has adjusted to the preschool fairly well; better than I expected. I saw the other kids doing their thing and it was difficult for me to imagine Andrew doing what they were doing, like sitting on the rug for circle time. But the teacher has assured me that Andrew will learn. The other kids weren't able to do those things at the beginning of the school year, she said. For Andrew, this is like the beginning of the year. It makes sense.

February 14, 2000

I've noticed that a lot of times Andrew stares into space for up to thirty seconds at a time. At first we thought it was funny and wondered "where he went." But his teacher started noticing him doing it at school as well. When I mentioned it to the pediatrician, she referred Andrew to a neurologist to have him tested for petty mal seizures. I know nothing about them and it's kind of scary.

[Author's note: I've since learned that these are called "petit mal" seizures, also known as an "absence seizure." Usually, a petit mal seizure involves a brief, sudden lapse of conscious activity. Each seizure lasts only seconds or minutes, but hundreds may occur each day. For more information, visit www.mayoclinic.com]

February 19, 2000

Andrew's EEG is scheduled for March 2. I'm doing better about it since I have educated myself about it. He is only supposed to sleep for four hours the night before the test. Then, they want him to lie down with electrodes stuck to his head. He may be asleep. If not, I doubt he'll lie still. I'll be glad to get this behind us.

March 1, 2000

Andrew has developed a low-grade fever. (Jesse's temperature reached 104.2 degrees on Monday.) They have postponed his EEG to next Thursday.

March 13, 2000

They did the EEG on the 9th. I just received a copy of the report. It states that "This electroencephalogram taken during wakefulness, drowsiness, and sleep was normal for age." In other words, it was a normal report. Thank You, Lord! I am so glad to have that behind us. What a nightmare this has been.

The night before the procedure Donald kept Andrew awake until midnight. We let him go to sleep. Then, I got him up at 4 a.m. and had to keep him awake. We watched a movie, played with toys, and had all the lights on. Actually, he did very well. He got pretty crabby after we checked into the hospital. I don't blame him. I was tired, too. The electrodes were stuck to a swimmer's cap that fit snugly over his head. He wasn't crazy about it, but they let me hold him. I was so glad when he finally fell asleep. I thought my arms were going to break. But it's behind us and everything looks to be fine. Of course, we still don't have a reason for why he does the "stares." That's another mystery.

March 15, 2000

Andrew has settled into the school routine. He is making progress in his ability to follow directions, answer simple questions, and partici- pate with his peers. He still doesn't use his own language very much but he does ask for help on occasion and requests snacks. He can also ride a tricycle. That's one of the things they were concerned about. I told them that the reason he couldn't ride a tricycle is that he didn't have one. They thought it was a problem with his gross-motor skills. I knew he could do it once he gave it a try.

April 20, 2000

I had to take Andrew to the doctor for a new problem. About six days ago, he suddenly started using the bathroom ten to twenty times a day. The doctor thinks it is psychogenic, that it's all in his head. She said to give it two weeks without paying any attention to the problem at home or at school. If it doesn't go away, we'll try medication.

May 18, 2000

We met with Andrew's therapists and teacher to see if he qualifies for the summer program. He does, but we have opted not to put him in it. It doesn't appear to be worth it with a change in teachers, therapists, and schedule for only six weeks of class. He has already met more than half of their goals for the year, so he is doing very well. The language therapist has given us some good tips on how to talk with him, to make the most of each conversation.

They have also given us a referral to a clinic that is part of the University of New Mexico (UNM) that deals with developmental delays in children. They are the specialists in our area. They can better answer some of our questions about expectations and which battles are the important ones. They may even be able to help us better diagnose what may be going on inside that little head of his so we can work with him better. It's the old dance of two steps forward and one step back.

Andrew stopped using the bathroom as much as he was, so we didn't have to put him on medication. I'm so glad. We have enough issues without adding any more.

Donald has had a taste of what it's like to take Andrew out in public and have people give you the "look" – the "you're raising a rude child" look. Andrew is as big as some five-year-olds but acts and talks like a two-year-old. We're learning to basically ignore those people. Andrew is a sweetheart. We couldn't love him more and who needs those people?

May 20, 2000

Mom commented recently about how well we are dealing with Andrew. I didn't do so well last night though. Jesse had his spring program at school. Andrew only made it through three songs and then started getting out of hand. Nothing worked. We told him he'd get a time-out if he didn't stop yelling, but then he began yelling that he wanted a time-out. Donald had to take him outside and missed the rest of the program. It was so frustrating. I was a little embarrassed, but mostly I was incredibly sad. Donald is just as frustrated and sad as I am. He hurts for our son.

I know that Andrew wasn't being disobedient or pushing the boundaries. He truly didn't understand and couldn't be quiet. But it makes me so sad because I want to be able to take him places like the library, a movie, or his brother's school program but I don't feel I can. He is too disruptive. We're getting a babysitter for Jesse's kindergarten graduation. It's going to be a long program and it starts late. Mostly, though, it's because of Andrew's behavior. He's been acting up at school a little more, too. He's gotten several time-outs there this past week. He tried to push his teacher away yesterday morning while I was still there talking with the teacher's aide. We have our hands full!

June 3, 2000

My frustrations with Andrew grew and grew today. It's confusing. I love him so much and want to protect him, but in a moment of anger, I want to hit him. I'm so frustrated! I'm frustrated at him, at his behavior, and especially at me. And I'm scared, too. What if he doesn't get any better? What if he stays delayed and behind?

As if all this wasn't enough, now there are vision problems. He is developing a lazy eye and is having a hard time seeing out of his right eye. We have an appointment with the specialist on Wednesday. I anticipate he will need an eye patch or glasses. I know Andrew will not like either and will probably react with more yelling and hitting.

June 8, 2000

We ordered glasses for Andrew yesterday. I hope we can convince him to wear them. He is far-sighted, and if the glasses don't fix the eye problem, he'll need surgery. The glasses should work though. With the eye doctor we've added another specialist to our list of doctors.

June 12, 2000

Andrew got his glasses today. He is wearing them and looks so cute. More important, he can see!

June 16, 2000

Jesse and Andrew went outside to play baseball this afternoon. They hadn't been out there for two minutes when I heard Andrew howl and start crying. Before I could respond, Jesse came in and as he passed me in the kitchen (not stopping or slowing down), he said very matter-of-factly, "I'm going to time-out." After I checked on Andrew, Jesse admitted that he had punched Andrew in the stomach. While I was talking with Jesse, Andrew came in, looked at Jesse and said, "Jesse, don't hit my Jesse." He stopped and thought about it (realizing that wasn't quite what he meant). Then he said, "Jesse, don't hit my Andrew." Jesse and I both had to grin at that one.

In some ways, they are learning to get along better, and Jesse is a bit more affectionate towards Andrew than he has been. In other ways, there's a lot more hitting going on. Andrew is getting harder and harder to "control"… or maybe it's my perception. I took them both to the dentist yesterday. Andrew threw such a loud fit. I was so embarrassed and felt so out of control. It's not that I want to control him as if he were a robot. I just wish he'd stop screaming in public. There is no reasoning with this child, especially when he's yelling that he wants a time-out and there's no place to give him one. Oh well, I guess that's why God has made him so incredibly adorable. It balances out somehow.

June 23, 2000

I just got a packet of information from the UNM Center for Development and Disability we were referred to. The information is mostly on autism but has some very interesting information about subgroups and related disorders. In my "spare time" I'm trying to learn a little more about PDD-NOS or Pervasive Development Disorders-Not Otherwise Specified. It's basically a diagnosis for children who do not fully meet the criteria of symptoms for the other PDD types (i.e., autism, Asperger's Disorder). These types are also known as autism spectrum disorder (ASD). All these different names are confusing.

Andrew has some of the symptoms but not all. The symptoms I noted in Andrew are resistance to change, difficulty in expressing needs, echolalic speech, tantrums, lack of eye contact, doesn't seem to feel pain, limited food preferences, limited cloth texture preferences, no imaginative play, and doesn't play with other children. Other symptoms of PDD that don't seem to apply to Andrew include preferring to be alone, spins objects, inappropriate attachment to objects, and poor gross-motor skills.

I'm really wrestling with how far I should take this. Do I try to figure out what's going on or do I wait and see what happens in the next year or two? I don't want to label Andrew, but I would like to know what to expect.

I told Donald that since Andrew is functioning (behaviorally) like a two-year-old, that's how I have been treating him. Not in a bad way. I'm just treating him as if he is just now learning that hitting is not okay … or yelling. It helps my expectations and, thus, the way I react. I just wish I had some assurances that we are doing the best we can and not making any huge mistakes … like too low expectations. Thus, our struggle continues.

Mom thinks we should try to figure out what is going on versus waiting to see. We need as much information as is available when making our decisions. However, that does not mean that we have to put labels on Andrew unless they are necessary to get him the help he needs. We must be careful because if we lock him into a label, we yoke him with our expectations rather than letting him do what he is led to do and is capable of doing. Mom is pretty smart.

June 27, 2000

The specialist told us today that Andrew's glasses aren't working the way they should. We have to patch his left eye for three weeks and are looking at surgery.

July 16, 2000

I've been doing some of the reading on PDD-NOS. I have a lot more research to do. I obviously can't answer all my questions by just reading a few books or articles. When Andrew has his good days, I see improvement and think that surely this will eventually pass. When he has his bad days (or moments), I get so frustrated. It was obvious on vacation that his behavior is not typical, and it hurts.

We've been on vacation with my family. Jesse finally began to play with his cousins, Brandon and Michael. Andrew just did his own thing. Uncle Jim asked how they might include Andrew. It was sweet of him to ask, but the bottom line is, there is nothing that can be done right now that we know of. Andrew plays next to other children, but not with them. The only exception is when he is playing some kind of sport like baseball or soccer, then he will play with someone else. Brandon didn't really like Andrew and complained to me about Andrew's hitting and not being nice. It was hard for Brandon to understand.

Andrew's temper tantrums are getting more frequent and more physical. He hits, kicks, pinches, throws things, and yells very loudly. We tried twice to go to a sit-down restaurant. Both times were disasters. We just have to let it go and realize that we won't be able to do that for a while.

I am anxious to get to the resource center in Albuquerque to do some more research. He is talking better but still has a long way to go, especially if he is to go to kindergarten in two years. He still likes *CNN Headline News*. I'm concerned about his eyes. At least the patch seems to help straighten out his eye some. I take him back to the doctor on Wednesday and we'll go from there. I'm not sure which to hope for: no surgery but continue wearing the patch or no patch but surgery. God knows best.

July 30, 2000

Andrew got two time-outs at church for shoving a kid. The teacher told him the first time that "we don't push," and Andrew said okay. He went over to apologize to the kid and gave him a hug. Two minutes later, he shoved him again. I had to explain to the teacher that Andrew was just going through the routine of apologizing but that he didn't really understand what he did wrong. This is the scary part for me. He is a big kid and the older he gets, the less patient people are with his behavior. He has no control of his impulses. It makes me wonder if I'm going to end up in all his Sunday School classes just to keep an eye on him.

August 13, 2000

If we really love God, we will obey Him. In some ways, the bigger "test" of that is Andrew. Love doesn't keep track of how many times we have to correct his behavior before we have "permission" to get really angry. He doesn't understand and all we can do is respond in gentleness and patience, persistence and consistency, and with a lot of prayer that one day, it will click for him and he'll understand. Oh, what a day that will be!

August 14, 2000

As I sit here at the park and watch the boys play, I have a sense of hope. I see improvement in Andrew. He is communicating better, and he did so well at the eye specialist this morning. We had him learn some symbols so it would be easier to test his vision. He learned them on the first try. This kid is smart! He has so much potential. I just know he'll be okay.

It is so nice to see Jesse and Andrew playing well together. It doesn't happen very often. I know Jesse wishes Andrew would play with him more. He doesn't really understand Andrew's behavior although we try to explain it to him as best we can.

August 24, 2000

It's the first day back at school. Andrew did great! His teacher said it was as if he'd never left. I'm so thankful. I've been stressing over what progress he might have lost over the summer when we decided to keep him home.

August 27, 2000

Today was my last day at my part-time job. I've been working at the church since Andrew was a year old. It was good to have something else to focus on besides him, but Donald and I feel that I'm needed at home more. So, now I am officially a stay-at-home mom again. The farewell reception went well, but Andrew stole the show. While the chairman of the personnel team was giving his little speech, Andrew came running up to the stool I was sitting on. So I put him on my lap, which lasted all of three seconds. I put him down, and he started to run back to Donald so I turned my attention back to the speaker. Next thing I know, everyone starts laughing. Andrew had run behind me and picked up one of the microphones and started to sing. It wasn't on so you couldn't hear him. He put it down and picked up another one. Donald had to come get him and carry him off while he was yelling, "No! No! Let go!"

I get embarrassed by Andrew's behavior. It's worse when he tantrums in front of total strangers and they glare at me. That's embarrassing, but I also want to punch them in the nose. Sometimes, I feel so judged. Even with well-intended friends, I can still be embarrassed. I guess my pride is on the line. Let's face it. I can't control my own kid. What kind of parent does that make me?

August 28, 2000

Note from school:

Well, our boy did very well today! Our SLP (speech-language pathologist) came and worked with us during snack. Our PT (physical therapist) worked with Andrew individually. Andrew tried getting up at snack and wasn't very happy with me when I made him sit back down. He hit me and, of course, he went to time-out. He was not a problem the rest of the day! He was just trying me. Had to see if I was still the same as last year. He slept about forty-five minutes today. He got to play on the computer, too.

September 7, 2000

Note from school:

Andrew had a very rough morning. He calmed down eventually, after a time-out, crying, and being comforted. He did the "stares" at least four different times this morning. He was definitely different. I can say that I have never seen him like this.

September 11, 2000

I am feeling so much stress with Andrew that I have been on the verge of tears for two weeks now. The range of emotions is incredible. I feel so grateful and excited about how well he is talking and communicating. Then, I feel so frustrated and sad over his behavior. I don't know what's going on with him. He doesn't want to be at school or church.

Yesterday, when I tried to drop him off in his Sunday School class, he began to yell and kept running out of the room. When I caught him and held him, he hit me so hard that my glasses flew across the table. I gave him a swat, which made him cry hard. But at least he stopped being abusive and could let me hold him and comfort him. When I gave him over to his teacher, he started yelling again. I had to make a run for it. I checked on him through the window a few minutes later and saw he was fine.

Today, he yelled all the way to school. It took five minutes to get him out of the van without forcing him. Last Thursday when I took him, it was the worst morning we had had in I can't remember how long. The teacher's note to me that day said he had a rough day. They had never seen him like that.

Last night, he did that thing again where he began crying hard and loud. It took nearly five minutes to calm him down, and his body was shaking so hard, it was almost like a seizure. It seems like a "night terror." It is so scary when he does that. This is the fourth or fifth time since he started doing it two weeks ago. I'm going to take him to the doctor tomorrow for a physical and to talk with her about it.

I don't know what's going on except my health is suffering. I get stress headaches just about every day now, mostly from Andrew yelling so loud. My stomach also gets upset and when I have to get up with him in the middle of the night, I don't sleep well after that. I feel tired all the time. Enough complaining. I know I need to take one day at a time and to always remember where my strength comes from. It's just so hard some times.

[Author's note: Night terrors are very different from regular nightmares. A few of the symptoms of night terrors are screaming, sweating, confusion, inability to explain what happened, inability to fully awake, difficult to comfort, and little or no memory of the event on awakening the next day. For more information, visit www.nightterrors.org]

September 12, 2000

My frustration level has gone even higher. I can't get Andrew in to see the pediatrician for at least two weeks. I did have time to go by the Center for Development and Disability to look at their resource center. I asked if anyone was around whom I could talk to, and it turns out the lady I've been playing phone tag with was in. She came down to talk with me. We talked for about fifteen minutes. It was so helpful. She said that the fact that Andrew has good days is great because it means there is potential and hope for improvement. The fact that we have so many questions means he is at least high functioning. If he wasn't, we would be more confident of what we had. I had the pediatrician's referral with me so the lady made a copy of it. If there is a cancellation, she'll call me. Right now, we are on a five-month waiting list for an evaluation. It was such good news, and it felt good just to be heard by someone.

September 18, 2000

Note from school:

Andrew did well today. He did get a little pushy with one of the students. We did see that, just today. He got a time-out and told us he was ready to get out of time-out. So we rewarded him appropriately. In other words, when he told us he was ready, we let him come back and join us. He also asked his classmate, with prompting from us, appropriately, if he could have the car he was playing with. All in all, it was a good day for him. He ate well and played hard.

September 21, 2000

Andrew's strabismus surgery was yesterday. We just got done with his post-op visit, and the doctor is very pleased. He said his eyes are perfectly straight. Praise God! He is almost himself today. Bouncy, happy, demanding. I love it. I have my hands full keeping him from rubbing his eyes but it's not bad. He even slept pretty well last night ... better than I did! I'm so relieved that it's over. I did much better than when he had his tubes put in. Donald was able to be there. The three of us watched television as Andrew got more and more drowsy. Then, instead of taking him from my arms like they did for the ear tubes, they just wheeled him off in his bed. It was so much easier.

September 27, 2000
Another happy birthday, Andrew.

Four years old. I've looked over many of the things I've written and all the things that happened last year. It's been quite a year, hasn't it? So many changes: doctor's appointments, tests, the glasses and surgery. Now, we've just gotten the phone call that the Center for Development and Disabilities will be evaluating you on October 10. I have my suspicions, sweet boy, but we'll soon know for sure. I don't understand everything that's going on, and I don't do everything right. But I love you so much and I'm proud of you. You are my sweet boy and you always will be.

Our Reality Check:
Autism Spectrum Disorder

❖

(September 2000 – December 2000)

September 28, 2000

Note from school:

Andrew did very well today. His birthday cupcakes were a big hit. An-drew did tell me "no" several times and tried to hit me once. He knows I do not tolerate either. He got time-out each time and was fine ... even told me he was sorry. This is a good sign! He is understanding and taking responsibility for his actions.

October 2, 2000

Andrew's eyes have aligned well, so he wears his glasses more will-ingly. He is doing better at playing and interacting, and almost seems like the other kids at times. At other times, though, he is very loud, obsessive, and throws temper tantrums without a known reason.

October 5, 2000

I took Andrew to McDonald's the other day to play and he threw a loud fit. A man sitting nearby talked rather sharply to Andrew, which made me mad. The man's back was turned to me so I refrained from saying anything to him. Still, it was rather embarrassing. I ended up carrying Andrew out while he struggled. He cried all the way home. I didn't leave because of the man or the worker staring. Andrew just needs to know he can't act that way and still get to play. I cried all the way home, too.

October 10, 2000

Andrew had his assessment today. He was in a good mood and was very cooperative. We were there for four hours: a little over two hours of testing and answering questions and half an hour for the therapists to meet and compare notes while we grabbed a bite to eat. Then, a little over an hour of question-and-answer time. Their diagnosis is that Andrew has an autism spectrum disorder – more specifically, PDD-NOS. In other words, it was what we suspected.

It has been difficult to express just what I feel … or rather, everything I'm feeling. I'm so glad that we finally know what we are dealing with, but I'm also so sad that we were right. As Donald said, we were holding on to the hope that he was just delayed; that in the end, he would become normal. Bottom line is, Andrew will never be "normal." The therapist says he doesn't have a language delay. Instead, he doesn't process or learn the same way other kids do. He will always learn differently. He most likely will have difficulty learning to read. She said his behavior would improve as his ability to communicate does (especially processing feelings), but until then it had to be endured. Don't let him hit, of course, but if he isn't hurting himself or others, let him go, was the advice we got.

Donald was able to ask questions I wouldn't have thought of – especially questions about the future. Some kids with ASD grow up and can have a full-time job or an apartment. They may require some services. Few of them marry and have a family. I guess it's hard for them to develop those kinds of relationships. In the shorter term, home schooling may not be a good option because of the need to be in a social environment, learning from others. The Center recommends twenty-five hours of therapy a week for someone Andrew's age. This is a great time (age) for intervention. I'm going to check into petitioning the school to let Andrew go four days a week. Some kids develop seizures around puberty. With our earlier concerns, Andrew may be susceptible to them. He could also develop into a fuller case of autism or he could develop to where some of the time he can be "mainstreamed" into regular classrooms. There is no way to tell at this time how he will develop.

The staff pointed out that Andrew has some real positive things going for him: He is trying to communicate and socialize; he has good days; his list of food preferences is not as limited as we thought; he is healthy; he got into an intervention program early; we love him and want what's best for him. (Apparently some parents aren't as loving and caring as Donald and I demonstrated. They commended us for that.) What else did they say? His vocabulary is largely "Disney language." He quotes movies because that's where he has learned most of his language, and he is trying to relate what he is experiencing to what he has learned from movies. That's an interesting concept. They seemed pleased with the relationship and interaction Andrew has with Jesse and even Stephen, from next door. He just needs to move it outside the home.

I can't help but wonder what this will mean to our family. Andrew being developmentally delayed is one thing. That diagnosis gave us hope of him "catching up" to his peers. To know we are dealing with a disorder is another thing. It sounds so final; so permanent. I think I'm still somewhere between denial and depression. It is one thing to suspect. It's another to have it confirmed. I watched Andrew today – smiling, giggling, running around and wrestling with the dog. He looked so normal! Surely this can't be right. He's just delayed. He is getting better. He is talking. I want so much for him to be delayed and not disabled. Yet, it occurs to me that my prayer is the same whether he is delayed or disabled. Lord, help me to help Andrew be the best person he can be and may he come to know You as Lord and Savior.

[Author's note: There are many terms to describe the same disorder: PDD, ASD, autism. Some are more widely recognized and accepted than others. I have found only one criterion for deciding which term to use to describe your child's diagnosis: use the one that will get you the help you need. If a doctor, therapist, or insurance company will only accept "autism," that's what you call it. If you find it easier to explain PDD, that will work, too. Our family has chosen to use the term ASD because it is comprehensive, yet generalized. For those who have a basic understanding of ASD, enough to ask us about it, we go on to explain that Andrew's specific diagnosis is Asperger Syndrome, as seen in future journal entries.]

October 12, 2000

Note from school:

Andrew had a really tough morning. He had to go to time-out several times for hitting. (He took himself the second time.) He wasn't at all happy at snack time. By lunch, he was fine. He did tell us he wanted to lie down, but he didn't sleep. He let us know he was unhappy this morning by his body language. He would walk "slumped over." It was really quite comical. Of course, we didn't laugh because that would not validate him letting us know how he felt. He is really a good little boy! It's so hard not to adore him. We've got to find out what his aversion to coming to school is. We're going to start a reward and prize chart for each student. I'll let you know how that's going. We will be working on "being nice" (i.e., not hitting, pushing or saying no) for Andrew.

October 13, 2000

I'm seeing Andrew through new eyes since the diagnosis. I guess before I never felt sure how much he understood or how much to expect. Now I feel more confident. It will always be a struggle to have realistic expectations but at least we know what we are dealing with. We are meeting with the school. Andrew will be going to preschool four days a week instead of two starting in a few weeks. In some ways, I feel like I'm losing my little boy. I never wanted him to be in preschool. Now, he'll be gone four full days, but what else can we do?

I feel bad for Mom and Dad and for Donald's parents. They are hurting for Andrew's diagnosis, but they are also hurting for Donald and me. They are both grandparents and parents. This has to be difficult for them in a way we can't understand yet.

Donald said he was able to have a good cry when he was with the praise band at church. They surrounded him, prayed for him and us, and just accepted his tears. I feel so blessed that Donald has never once told me that Andrew's problems are in my head. He has agreed with me from day one that something wasn't right. Not all husbands are that understanding. I'm glad he could cry and admit his hurt. I'm still waiting for my good cry. I've shed some tears the past few days but I feel like something is holding back the flood that I know has to come some time.

October 24, 2000

I had to get Andrew into the doctor's office today. He's had an increase in bed-wetting for the past week. He is also badly constipated. He is taking Lactolose syrup. Pretty gross, if you ask me. I don't remember signing up for this part.

November 8, 2000

It is so obvious to us that Andrew is intelligent, but it is equally obvious that he can't express it. If we ask questions in a certain way, he can answer them. But if you ask basically the same thing and just reword it, he doesn't have a clue what you're talking about. Everything about his learning makes us feel like we are in slow motion. When he is home, we just go along with our routine and it is easy to "forget" about his disorder because we don't see other kids.

Jesse is getting more frustrated with Andrew. Jesse wants him to play with him, but Andrew usually doesn't. Jesse can't understand why I won't "make Andrew play." When Andrew does play, it is usually very rough and one of them (mostly Jesse) ends up getting hurt. Or Andrew doesn't play by the rules Jesse puts down. I think some of our frustration is really sadness in seeing the boys growing further apart and knowing there is little we can do about it except praise and be thankful for the times they do get along.

[Author's note: When dealing with a child with special needs, it is important to recognize the toll on siblings. Many siblings deal with anger: anger that the special child gets extra attention, sympathy, and what appears to be special favors. There is also anger that comes with the child's embarrassing behaviors. A sibling may understand why things are the way they are; yet, the sense of unfairness can be so strong that when anger rises, the sibling feels guilty for feeling angry. This anger and guilt must be dealt with before it turns into bitterness or resentment.

We sought counseling for Jesse when he began to exhibit extreme anger towards me. The counselor assured us that Jesse's anger was largely due to Andrew's circumstances and that I was Jesse's "safe" outlet for his anger. The counselor was able to give us ideas to help Jesse deal with his feelings concerning his brother.]

November 24, 2000

I am drained from Andrew's yelling and Jesse's arrogant disrespect. If it's not one, it's the other – and sometimes it's both. I hope the written report on Andrew's evaluation is waiting for us. I've got to get hooked up with a support group. Andrew may not be "all that bad," but it's all I can handle. I'm not strong enough to handle it any more. I've heard a few comments of how I should be glad that Andrew "isn't that bad" and "at least he talks." On one hand, those comments make me feel guilty. I should be more grateful than I am, especially right now. On the other hand, they make me so mad. I'm mad at unfeeling people who judge me on something they don't understand. I'm mad that people are rude and feel superior. I'm angry that Andrew can't help the way he is. I'm angry at myself for caring about other people's opinions so much. That is something I've got to get over. Besides, just because Andrew talks doesn't mean we don't struggle, get frustrated, or feel hurt.

December 3, 2000

This is a list I sent to Andrew's teachers at church to give them some ideas that we have found helpful in relating to Andrew.

1. In your overall perception of Andrew, consider him like you would a child who is two years old. He is learning right from wrong. He needs the patience and discipline given to a child who doesn't mean to do wrong but needs to learn – not the punishment of one who deliberately disobeys. Time-outs work well.

2. Eye contact is very important. You may have to touch his arm or say "Andrew, look at me" in order to get his attention. Be sure he makes eye contact with you. Otherwise, he will not truly hear you.

3. Use short, clear directions. He can only comprehend and respond to one-step directions.

4. Use "first, then" statements. For example, if he wants to play but it's time to color, say, "First we will color. Then we will play."

5. He has a limited attention span. Don't be surprised if he spends only a minute coloring or listening to a story. As long as he is not disrupting the class, we ask your patience in letting him do his own thing. He is getting better in this area!

6. Sometimes Andrew gets overstimulated and needs to regroup. He usually moves off by himself, away from everyone, or clings to something that offers comfort such as his blanket or a teacher's lap/shoulder in which to hide his face.

7. A routine or structure is very helpful in getting him to transition between activities smoothly.

8. Andrew is quite visual. He understands what you want quicker if you show him as well as telling him, rather than only telling him.

9. He is good at answering yes/no questions (although not always accurately). You will need to help him answer open-ended questions but these are the kinds of questions that help him learn best.

10. His temper-tantrums often come when he is tired, hungry, or over-stimulated. They begin with yelling. Distractions often work combined with telling him (eye contact) that he doesn't need to yell. He can also become distressed if he says something to someone and the person does not respond. For example, if he says "thank you," he will continue saying it (louder each time) until the person says "you're welcome."

[Author's note: Most people you come into contact with want to help you and your child, but they are unclear on how to go about it. A letter is a good means of communicating vital information. Be sure to include specific ways they can relate to your child. Everyone benefits from the information, especially if it is in written form so it can be referred back to as needed.]

December 7, 2000

Andrew has had a cough and lots of congestion for about a week. He's got a low-grade fever and a very infected left ear. We are back on Amoxicillin, which he takes better than the Augmentin. Augmentin smells like pineapple and tastes nasty.

December 12, 2000

Note from school:

Andrew rested but didn't sleep. Today after lunch, we had first graders come to our room for recess. He went to the restroom and I followed him. He didn't even get in there to take care of business when he walked out, gave a little cry, dropped the toy that was in his hand, and turned white as a sheet. I grabbed him and he just went limp. I asked him if his tummy hurt and he said no. He didn't want to get up from my lap, so we just sat there on the floor by the restroom for a while. I asked him if he wanted me to hold him and he said he wanted me to. The color in his face finally came back and he was able to go sit with everyone else. Don't know what that was all about, but wanted you to know. He hasn't had a bit of trouble the rest of the day.

Christmas 2000

Andrew is 43 inches tall these days. He takes comfort in repetitive activities, such as putting the same puzzle together over and over or repeating movie lines to himself. He is beginning to use pronouns. He still does not like for his head or face to be touched. His favorite toy is Larry Boy. We had our Christmas Eve service at home with guitar and singing since Andrew can't sit in church without being disruptive. He did try to sing with us.

December 30, 2000

It seems to me that Andrew has regressed the past few days. He seems more whiny and argumentative, and is basically living on applesauce and peanut butter and jelly sandwiches. The one saving grace is that he is sleeping at night. We mailed the dues to the Autism Society. I subscribed on-line to a free newsletter and we are looking into hippo-therapy (therapy on a horse). I'm hoping the monthly support group will start soon.

Introducing New Hope: Hippotherapy

❖

(January 2001 – March 2001)

January 8, 2001

Andrew had an interesting break. His expressive language is showing some improvement but we have noticed some decline in his behavior. He has been less cooperative and more inclined to temper tantrums. He is interacting with others less and seems to be more "ritualistic."

It may be that since his days have not been consistent, he has turned some things he can control into rituals. (He lines up the videos in a particular order, and he won't sleep until he has the exact toys in a pile on a particular spot in his bed.) Perhaps that will change as we get back into our school routine. I hope so! He is really unhappy at the thought of going back to school, so it may take a few days to adjust back.

January 10, 2001

Andrew and I just got back from the on-site consultation for hippo-therapy at Skyline. It was incredible. Andrew rode a horse and was grinning and laughing the whole time. The therapist that worked with him said that within minutes of riding, they could see him getting more organized in his sensory processing and orientation to what was going on. I don't understand it all, but even I could see something was different about him. We are going to start the therapy next week. He'll go for one hour once a week on Wednesday mornings. We've arranged for a morning time slot, so we will leave the house at the same time as for school the other four days. That way it won't break up the morning routine.

The therapist told me that while it was good that the school was working with Andrew on certain motor skills like trying to cut with scissors, she would be taking a different approach that will actually help Andrew more than what the school was doing. It was all new to me so she said that they will educate Donald and me as we go and give us things we can do at home. I'm really excited about this find. The OT (occupational therapist) noted concerns in the following areas: sensory processing (aversion to tactile stimulation), transition abilities, attention span, and sleep issues. Nothing new there, really.

[Author's note: While hippotherapy proved to be very beneficial to Andrew, there is no evidence to suggest it helps all children. As with any therapy, it is a trial-and-error process to discover what works for the individual child.

All ASD children deal to some degree with sensory integration issues which include the tactile sense, the proprioceptive sense, and the vestibular sense. For more information, I recommend the book *The Out-of Sync Child* written by Carol Stock Kranowitz and *Asperger Syndrome and Sensory Issues* by Brenda Smith Myles and her colleagues.]

January 11, 2001
Progress report from the school's speech therapist:
    Andrew has made excellent progress toward his communication and language goals this quarter. He seems to improve in spurts and demonstrates an understanding of new concepts seemingly "suddenly" or "out of the blue." This may indicate that he is absorbing information and (over time) is conceptualizing new information that he then uses when given an opportunity. He is not consistent with the use of these concepts (yet), but we will continue to work toward greater consistency. Andrew's use of novel utterances during therapy activities is encouraging. This is indicative that he is bringing his own ideas to the activity.

January 13, 2001
We had a rough couple of days with the boys – each for their own reasons. Andrew is driving us nuts asking to ride the horse every half hour. He threw fits about going to school on Thursday and Friday. Hopefully, we'll get into a routine soon.

January 19, 2001

Andrew had his first speech/language session during hippotherapy. They used picture symbols to help organize and plan the session. Andrew did well. He will alternate meeting with the OT and the SL (speech-language) each week.

[Author's note: There are many therapies available for children with many different needs. We chose to focus on the hippotherapy. Hindsight has proven it was one of the best things we did for Andrew, in addition to early intervention. It suited his needs perfectly. For more information on hippotherapy, visit www.americanequestrian.com/hippotherapy.htm]

January 23, 2001

Note from school:

Wow! What a day! We're not sure if it was the fire drill first thing this morning or the fact that Andrew is smart enough to know his parents are going to be back this evening, but did we have an interesting day! After the fire drill, we went to physical therapy. He got to roll and crawl, jump, etc., and that really got his motor running. He was so active, talkative, and singing all day long that at rest time, he crashed hard! We did our normal things, like put in a video to see if we could wake him gently. Nothing seemed to work. After about 30-45 minutes he woke up. No, it was more like an hour. He did fine. Last time he woke up crying. I think this had to be the most active day I have ever encountered with Andrew. He is a great kid. Even with all of his adventures today, we love him even more!

Donald and I went away for three nights without the kids. We haven't done that since right after Jesse was born. It was difficult to leave, but I got over that real quick. I think all parents, but especially those with kids with special needs, need to have time away on a regular basis. Still, it's good to be home.

January 25, 2001

Andrew had his second hippotherapy session yesterday. He really loves to ride the horse. I have been amazed. He will sit forwards, backwards, sidewise, and even lie down on his stomach on the horse. A few times, the therapist had the horse trot longer than Andrew wanted to go and he got upset, but she pushed him just past his threshold and then he was fine with the various sensations he was experiencing. It is amazing what they are able to do.

Basically, we are working on his sensory integration, which we feel may be at the root of his disorder. The interplay among our various senses is complex, and organizing the sensory input is necessary in order for us to make appropriate responses to the environment. For Andrew, the ability to respond to incoming sensations hasn't developed as efficiently as it should. His neurological system is disorganized and unable to interpret all the sensory information that comes in. The hippotherapy guides him through activities that challenge his ability to respond appropriately to sensory input by making a successful, organized response … all while riding the horse. We have noticed that his articulation improves while riding and he has been making adjustments in his responses to almost sliding off the horse.

The two therapists who work with him are very optimistic that they will be able to help him. Yesterday, the OT said that she loves working with kids like Andrew because they are bright and fun, and it is just a matter of helping him get organized so that the real "him" could shine.

January 28, 2001

Andrew is my baby. I feel protective of him, and his disabilities only make me want to protect him more. I feel proud of how well he has been doing. He is talking so much better and seems to be more aware of what's going on around him. He is smart. I know he is, and others tell me that they can see it, too. He isn't retarded. He is still a small boy. Some day his talents will be even more obvious. That makes me proud. But those "good" days seem so far and few between. His behavior can change so quickly.

It has been like living with a two-year-old for three years. You say "no" and he screams … loudly! Last Friday after we dropped Jesse off at a friend's house for a sleepover, I tried to take Andrew to the grocery store. I had only five items on the list and a storm was coming. It was just a quick trip. But he threw one of his temper tantrums. I couldn't reason with him. I finally had to put the bread back, return the cart and go home – all the while, he is screaming, kicking, and hitting at me. It was humiliating. Everyone from the produce section through the bakery and deli was staring. It was all I could do to keep from crying. Andrew did cry, and he screamed all the way home.

January 31, 2001

The OT at Skyline wants to do "brush therapy." She feels Andrew is tactile defensive. He only wears sweat pants with an elastic waist. He has to have his socks pulled up to his knees. He doesn't like light touch or strangers touching him. I don't know if it will help him eat new foods or not.

[Author's note: Brush therapy is also known as "Touch-Pressure Technique." For instructions on brush therapy, visit www.preemiemum. com/touchpressure_technique_.htm. This therapy is to be used under the guidance of an occupational therapist or physical therapist.]

February 8, 2001

Note from school:

Andrew had a difficult day. There were many "no's." We took care of it through time-outs. It is the day after Wednesday. Could be he would just prefer to be on that horse! Thank you so much for the straws. That's one thing we really use a lot. Andrew calls straws, strawberries. "Mrs. B., I need a strawberry for my milk." We always correct him but we still think it's pretty cute.

February 9, 2001

Note from school:

Andrew had another "no" day. We had several time-outs ... a little tantrum on the last time-out. He threw his glasses and that was when he knew that he had upset me! He had to stay in time-out a little longer and missed snack. But that was his choice. After that, he was as good as gold! He really had a good day after that. I told him, "Andrew, you can never throw your glasses again, ok?" He said, "Okay, Ms. B." And then we gave each other a hug. I hope we are through with this part of our "growing."

February 13, 2001

Andrew's speech is noticeably improved! He is starting to talk in complete sentences on a regular basis and initiating some conversation. He loves to ask "what are you doing?" and then echoes your response. While getting his pajamas on, he did about five seconds of arm flapping. (I think he was excited about snack time.) Getting ready to brush his teeth, he rocked sideways for about five seconds. He wants to roll in the blanket several times a day now.

February 14, 2001

The hippotherapy started fine, but he became overstimulated while on the horse. He shut down and didn't want to cooperate with the therapist after that. He was lying on his back on the horse followed by sitting sideways.

February 15, 2001

Note from school:

Andrew did well right up 'til rest time. He was not going to rest without singing or kicking something or whatever. So needless to say, he didn't rest. He wanted my chocolate pudding today at lunch. He kept saying, "Chocolate, Ms. B?" I didn't realize he meant the pudding, so I got some chocolate milk out. I said, "Is this what you want?" "No, Ms. B., Chocolate." Oh, my pudding? "Yeah," he said. He ate it all and savored every spoonful! It was Hunt's fat free chocolate pudding. Also, he got really stopped up today when he was lying down. He sniffed and sniffed, so maybe he was just uncomfortable lying down.

February 19, 2001

Andrew got the stomach flu on Saturday. His stomach finally settled down around three in the morning. I think I got a total of three hours sleep. Andrew and I slept on the floor of the boys' room so we could make fast tracks to the bathroom. He did so well, though. He learned to say "bowl" when he needed to throw up so he could do it in the bowl and not on the floor. It was a victory!

February 22, 2001

Andrew is finally well! He pointed to my watch and said "what's that?" I said, "It's my watch." "Watch?" "Yes, it's a clock people wear." He pointed to the clock on his dresser and said, "There's another clock." What a great exchange and transferring of thoughts! It was very exciting. I suppose most people would think I am nuts for getting so excited, but most people don't understand my Andrew. I went to school this morning for training in the brushing program along with three staff from the school.

February 25, 2001

Andrew picked out his own clothes, took his pajamas off, and put his clothes on all by himself. He even fixed the tag on his shirt. He had a flash card with pigs on it. He counted each pig until he came up with the correct total. He did that with several cards. It's the first time we have seen him count like that. I love these little victories.

March 1, 2001

Andrew ran a fever again earlier this week. He became very disorganized around dinnertime and stayed that way throughout the night. The bath water was "too hot." He did excessive spinning and rolling and wanted to "talk" but didn't know about what. He didn't sleep well and needed physical contact to calm down. I've noticed that after he has been sick, it can take a full week for him to get back to "normal."

March 2, 2001

Therapy went very well this morning. His echolalia is more pronounced when he is feeling okay. As he gets disorganized, his speech breaks down into whining, yelling, and slurred speech.

I think that there is within me the belief that Andrew is going to get better. I wonder if I'm fooling myself. The owner of Skyline spent a lot of time explaining some things to me while Andrew had his session. She said that Andrew will probably always have bad days. Hopefully, there won't be that many. The good days are his potential. They represent who he can become. She said the goal of the therapy is to help his body learn how to organize itself so that he can be an independent, fully functioning adult. Otherwise, he could slide into more autistic-like behavior. If his body doesn't learn how to function properly, it will shut down in self-defense. She said he isn't trying to pull anything on us (like last night when he was so disorganized, whining, and needed physical contact to sleep).

The thing that gets me is what I just read … that sensory integration dysfunction isn't cured by occupational therapy. It just makes it easier for the child to function. I'm not sure I have properly grieved for the diagnosis. I wonder if I have accepted that this is permanent. My head knows that this isn't going to go away. It will get better but it won't disappear. My heart is holding out for something better.

March 3, 2001

Last night was worse than Thursday night with Andrew screaming and not knowing what he wanted. I slept on the floor with him. He woke several more times yelling and scared but immediately calmed down when he saw me. During the day, he yelled a lot and was quite argumentative.

I picked up a weighted blanket. Andrew likes it on his legs and waist. It almost seems too heavy, though. We've done a lot of rolling in the regular blanket and playing football. He didn't want to be tackled, though.

March 7, 2001

It was a good, steady therapy today. The OT gave us a list of vestibular activities to do two-three times a day for five-ten minutes each without letting Andrew get overstimulated. It is supposed to help him regulate or modulate his system. We're also supposed to do deep pressure once an hour if possible.

March 9, 2001

Major victory! Andrew woke up this morning out-of-sync, crying, demanding, etc. He seemed to reach a threshold and then started sobbing. He let me hold him tight with the weighted blanket on his legs and comfort him. I could feel his body relax. Within fifteen minutes, he was eating, calm, and wanting to go to school. He had a good day – only a little out of it in the morning.

March 11, 2001

We bought a mini-trampoline. Andrew loves jumping on it and seems to be able to regulate himself. He hasn't asked to do the blanket roll for several days. He has slept through the night the last several nights. I'm so glad!

March 12, 2001

I am so angry and frustrated. "I love you, Andrew, but I hate your autism!" And once again I hear my friend Penny's question from that first session when I said Andrew had been diagnosed with ASD, "And what does that mean?"

What does it mean? Andrew's sweet face looms in front of me. I think of all the troubling behaviors that have led us to seek a diagnosis: the research, the testing, the confirmation of what we already knew and dreaded in our hearts. I think of the uncertainty of his future … and mine. What does it mean?

It means I have a trampoline in my living room. It means I always have extra applesauce and honey on hand. It means I pray every night that he will sleep so I can. It means a screaming temper tantrum is sure to follow hearing the word "no." It means I had another toy car thrown at me and he wouldn't stay in his room for time-out. It means more new activities to do every day, a new schedule, and the guilt when I don't keep it. It means going crazy from hearing the *Thomas the Tank Engine* theme song sung loudly and out of tune for the fiftieth time. It means not being able to take him out in public without having someone stare. It means I'm tired and I have a headache. It means I've lost track of how far he has come and how blessed we are.

I've decided it doesn't really matter what crisis a person faces. At some point, we all have to ask ourselves, "And what does that mean?" It's very personal, yet we must recognize where we are if we are ever going to be able to move forward. Right now, I'm at the point where I'm going to have a good cry, try to get some sleep, and start again tomorrow.

March 18, 2001

We visited my parents in Arizona for a few days last week. Andrew did very well. He didn't have any major tantrums. His sleep was restless but I may have heard him so much because he was on the floor by my bed. Today, he is irritable and whiny, and none of the "tricks" have helped. It's easier to just give him what he wants. Mom noticed that Andrew's eye contact has improved. It is sometimes spontaneous but is good when you ask him for it. He prefers cartoon movies to those with real people. He loved watching the trains that run behind their house, which is no surprise. He is obsessed with *Thomas the Tank Engine*.

[Author's note: In raising all children, you must choose your battles wisely. This becomes extremely important when dealing with a child with special needs. Each family must decide for itself which behaviors can be tolerated and which behaviors must be dealt with. One classic symptom of ASD is a resistance to change. We have found that we could not tackle more than two troublesome behaviors at a time. We had to prioritize the areas Andrew had difficulty with and work on the most important one until he learned what was expected. His safety and the safety of others remain a priority.]

March 20, 2001

Jesse asked Andrew if he wanted to play soccer. Andrew said, "Sure. I have to finish my numbers." He lined up his numbers and said, "Okay, Jesse. I'm ready to play soccer now." Wow! We are amazed at how well he is speaking in complete sentences relevant to the situation.

March 21, 2001

Andrew had a fantastic therapy session this morning. The weather was so beautiful that he got to ride his horse outside. They took a twenty-minute walk and he commented on everything – the trees, dogs, other horses, and the "horse's house." He didn't use any "Disney speech." We brought his therapy ball home today; a big, red ball he can roll on. We had a tough time getting him to settle down for bed.

March 23, 2001

Last night was awful. Around dinnertime, Andrew complained of something hurting. By 7:30, he was pulling at his ear. He woke up at 9:00 crying and screaming. His fever went up to 102 degrees. Finally, around 4:30 in the morning, his ear drum burst. He could actually sleep after that. His right ear is severely infected. The doctor is giving him Ceclor.

Trying More New Things: Brush Therapy, Diet, Speech Clinic

❖

(March 2001 – August 2001)

March 26, 2001

Andrew is keeping me running these days but he is doing so well. We are pleased with how well he is talking and behaving. Definite improvement! He is easily into the three-year-old range, which doesn't seem like much for a four-and-a-half-year-old but it is still improvement.

His occupational therapist has put him on a "sensory diet" at home. We have a mini-trampoline, therapy ball, and sit-n-spin in our living room. We have to do so many exercises for so long a day but no more or else he gets overstimulated. It is working pretty well. He is sleeping most nights and doesn't run down the hall and throw himself into the wall any more. (He thought that was fun.) Today, we started the "brush therapy." I literally brush his body every one and a half to two hours while he is awake.

March 27, 2001

This is the second day of brushing. He tolerates the brushing well but doesn't really like the compressions. This therapy seems to make Andrew very tired. His OT said it's not unusual for a child to sleep more and that he may not be interested in other sensory things (ball, trampoline) because of all the input from the brushing. This is Andrew's spring break, so we're able to let him rest more.

March 28, 2001

Andrew got overstimulated during therapy. The SL walked the horse quietly and after seven minutes or so, Andrew was able to reorganize and refocus on the therapy. That's the first time something like that has happened. The school has told me that Andrew is now able to cut paper in half once he is oriented to placing the scissors in his hands. He needs cues to stay focused on cutting. He can copy letters and marks, and he is showing greater flexibility in risk taking or trying new activities.

April 1, 2001

Andrew sang with the preschool choir in church today. We were very proud that he didn't run around the stage and play with the microphones. He stayed with the group. But the more I watched, the sadder I felt. He didn't move his feet, but he kept swaying his body and staring up at the high ceiling. Once in a while, he would sing a word or two. At one point, he lay down flat on the floor. (He does that in the store a lot.) Donald had to go up and get him to stand up again. It made us realize just how far he still has to go.

It made me feel somewhat afraid for him. He was cute. But it won't be cute much longer. He is doing better with "what is this" and "where is that" questions but doesn't have a clue about "when," "why" or "how" questions. Another thing is that even though he rides a horse once a week, just driving down the road, he can't tell a horse from a cow. We still don't know what's going on in his mind other than when he wants something. I guess this has been the "one step back" after feeling so positive the last month. I hate not knowing what the future holds for him.

April 2, 2001

I had a battle getting Andrew to school after being off last week for spring break. It was a nightmare. He cried and screamed. I had to pull him out of the van, and he cried all the way to the room. Luckily, he did fine once he was there. We've changed brushing to doing it on his bare skin rather than through his shirts. Also, we are doing jumps that pull him high by his hands in place of compressions. He likes the changes!

April 5, 2001

The OT confirmed that while sensory integration was an important factor in helping Andrew, it can't "fix" the autistic spectrum part. For example, the trouble we have with transitions. He will always need extra time to process any changes and actually make those changes from one activity to another. Their goal with the therapy is to teach him to do it independently without the prompts from us. So we are working on how we get Andrew moving along … especially in the morning. It takes more time now but with the goal of it paying off in the future.

April 6, 2001

Summary report from Skyline speech-language therapist:

Andrew generally needs time when he first arrives at therapy to organize to the new environment. He likes to play with magnetic letters and numbers. He also does well when allowed to jump on the trampoline for specified amounts of time. Andrew uses "Disney talk" when his system is disorganized and his language is hard to coordinate. Picture symbols and line-drawing plans for the therapy session have been used with moderate success.

When Andrew's system is too disorganized at the start of the session to attend to a plan, modified amounts of movement are given to calm his body and the plan is then addressed. Andrew was able to review his plan at the end of the last session and discuss and check off the activities he had completed. This was a very big step. After his sensory system regulates (generally after the first ten minutes of input), he exhibits increased organization in his language and is able to respond to clinicians' queries. He still uses approximately 50% echolalia patterns.

April 7, 2001

Andrew slept poorly last night. He was sick to his stomach at 2:30 a.m., possibly from drainage. He didn't have a fever. We went to the Urgent Care Clinic and found out that both ears are infected. During the night, Andrew told Donald, "My tummy is scared." He did very well at the Urgent Care – didn't really acknowledge the doctor or nurses but he did follow their directions.

He can't really tell us how he feels, but we are learning his "code." A few weeks ago, he was sick at his stomach. He told Donald, "my tummy scared." He uses the word "scared" to mean scared, not feeling well, or that he's not sure about something.

Jesse's birthday party was at Chuck-E-Cheese right after we went to Urgent Care. Andrew was easily distracted and whining, not feeling well but able to play. I made a new weighted blanket. It weighs the same as the blanket we were borrowing (4 lbs.), but the weight is distributed over a larger area so it doesn't feel as heavy. He loves the *Veggie Tales* slipcover we made for it.

April 10, 2001

Summary report for Skyline occupational therapist:

Andrew is responding well to the [brush therapy] program. He is show-ing signs of a decrease in his defensiveness through greater ease in his moth-er's ability to brush his teeth, decreased fidgeting with clothing, increased at-tention to tasks, and decreased occurrences of running off. Andrew's parents have found a strong correlation between Andrew's improved ability to settle into requested tasks and a change in their regulation of his activity.

Andrew is more interactive with his brother in play activities. His play has decreased in its frantic and unfocused nature to calmer and more focused periods of play. Occurrences of waking in the night are decreasing and he is able to settle into sleep much easier. Transitions out of the house to school and therapy continue to be difficult, yet once he has arrived, he is able to transi-tion with greater ease. Following verbal directives has been one of the greatest challenges for Andrew's parents at home. There has been significant progress with this during treatment sessions. Andrew's greatest need appears to be the allowance of time and information. Attention shifts are very difficult for him. Verbally and/or visually presenting information for what the next task is and when he will be expected to stop and follow the instructions has allowed An-drew time and information to process the need to shift his attention. Andrew is able to follow this with no resistance approximately 60% of the time.

April 11, 2001

Andrew had a rough day. He woke up out of sorts even though he slept well. He didn't want to ride the horse. He cried, hid his face in my jacket, and yelled "no." We had to make him get on the horse and hold him there because he was, at one point, literally on the side of the horse. As we walked, he became less agitated. It was amazing! After five minutes, he was more organized and cooperative. He moved into a lot of Disney speech to help with the inner organization.

Jesse was able to ride on the horse with Andrew after he settled down. Even though he never made eye contact with the SL, he heard her and cooperated. Andrew never got completely organized but it was an improvement over the morning. We still had a tough afternoon and evening but, again, not as bad as the morning.

I'm glad Jesse got to ride the horse. He doesn't really understand that it isn't all fun-and-games for Andrew; that it is therapy and hard work. All he sees is Andrew getting to ride a horse. He doesn't say it often but I know he thinks it's not fair. We try to point out that Jesse gets to do things Andrew doesn't, like go to a friend's house or ride a bike. We try to give him special one-on-one time with Daddy or Mommy. I so hope it's enough.

April 17, 2001

Andrew is something else. He is already as tall as Jesse was at age five. He is a big kid! He is still doing the horse therapy and it is helping. I can see changes in him while we are there, and the therapists have been wonderful to give us information and ideas. It is a slow process. Some days I feel so frustrated, but other days are good. They have recommended he go two days a week instead of one.

He is very close to being able to count to twenty. He is talking in sentences although they are choppy; not fluid. He is getting much better at identifying things. For example, he can tell us what he ate for lunch, what toys he played with, or what he sees out the window. That is exciting.

He is totally in love with *Thomas the Tank Engine*. Right now, I'm learning all I can about the nutritional aspect of the disorder and trying to get a plan for how to handle this summer when he isn't in school. There is so much to do.

April 18, 2001

We had an appointment with the pediatrician, which was interesting. First, Andrew's ears are fine. She gave us a referral to see the ENT for an ear test to determine if tubes are needed again. Second, we discussed vitamin B therapy. She recommends trying the gluten-casein-free diet (GFCF diet) first.

I asked about Andrew seeing a developmental pediatrician. She thought he had already seen one through the Center for Development and Disability. She recommended asking other parents if they know of a doctor who treats autism as a medical condition. She explained the difference between a medical and a developmental condition. For something to be "medical," it has to be a condition that is treatable or can be "fixed." It is "developmental" if it is a condition that can't be "fixed." (No wonder I'm having problems with the insurance company.) There aren't really any tests to diagnose autism. For food sensitivities, the best "test" is trial-and-error diets. The same is true for vitamins. This sure would be a lot easier if there was a "test."

[Author's note: Many children with ASD have demonstrated improvements in behavior and communication skills while adhering to the GFCF diet. For more information, visit www.gfcfdiet.com]

April 30, 2001

We are slowly stopping the brush therapy. It doesn't appear to have done a lot of good. We can't see much change, but Andrew's OT believes that it did help some. What she thinks is happening is that we need to work on his emotional response to touch. His deeply ingrained reaction to touch is fear – whether the touch itself is painful or not. She thinks that touch isn't as painful to him any more but that we haven't retrained the emotional response. It's fascinating albeit frustrating. It will be difficult to retrain him, because he doesn't fear my touch. Others will have to help work with him.

I took him to the eye doctor this week as a follow-up to the surgery. His eyes are aligned well but his stigmatism has changed so we're getting new lenses put in his eyeglass frames. Next month, it's the ENT doctor to do another tympo-something test to see if Andrew needs tubes put back in his ears.

We signed both boys up for swim lessons the last two weeks of June. I received special permission to be in the pool with Andrew, if needed, so that he could be in the preschool class and not with the babies. I've assured them that if I'm not needed, I will back off. It will be interesting to see how he does in a "normal" class.

Our insurance has approved Andrew going to hippotherapy two times a week. We'll begin that next week. The OT suggested that the behavioral difficulties we've been experiencing for the last week or so may be caused by changes in routine and the forced adjustment from long-sleeve to short-sleeved shirts because of the warmer weather. Andrew has had only one incident of waking up from a nightmare (disorganized) in a month. He wakes up if he has lost his blanket, his toys were moved, or the dimmer light goes off. He is scared of the dark and the nightlight isn't enough. He needs the overhead light on to feel safe.

May 2, 2001

Andrew rode bareback on the horse today. He had his socks around his ankles for five minutes while on the horse. It took two minutes after he got off the horse before he thought to pull them up. This was quite exciting because he is always pulling at his socks, stretching them up to his knees. We haven't been able to get him to stop doing that.

May 6, 2001

Both of Andrew's Sunday School teachers told me how well Andrew is doing. They noted his improved speech, social interaction, and participation. They are impressed! I love getting good news.

May 9, 2001

I explained to Andrew's OT about the various persons commenting on Andrew's improvement but that he seems to have regressed in behavior at home. He is more demanding, quicker to yell, throw tantrums, hit. We concluded it could be his diet. He may be hypoglycemic (myself, Grandma, and Aunt Paula are), and his blood sugar level may drop after he gets home from school. He needs more proteins and deep-pressure massage often. I am concerned about his nutrition since he is taking himself off most dairy products. He has not been drinking much milk lately and hasn't requested cheese for quite some time. He also doesn't want yogurt any more. We are trying to find a nutritionist.

May 11, 2001

Andrew is on yet another round of antibiotics. He has an ear infection, conjunctivitis, and is quite congested. In other words, he is miserable. I found out that a two-week treatment for overgrowth of yeast in the intestines is available at the health food store. We're going to try it because I've read in numerous places how antibiotics can kill off the good bacteria (flora) in the intestines. It is recommended that we try to get that worked on first, and then introduce the diet. I believe his appointment with the ENT doctor is in two weeks.

Andrew is totally obsessed with *Thomas the Tank Engine*. He wants me to buy the diesel engine from the movie. I keep telling him I don't have the money but when I do (next week), I'll get it for him. Every day when I pick him up from school, he asks if I have diesel. Yesterday, when he got in the van, he found a penny. He handed it to me and said, "Here, Mom. Here money for diesel." Sure enough, that afternoon he wanted to know if I had bought diesel. He is one smart boy ... if very focused.

May 22, 2001

Tonight Andrew wrote the whole alphabet in upper-case letters. He did a great job. We knew that he copied whatever letter they were working on at school, but we didn't know he could write them on his own. Donald thinks Andrew was "more alert" tonight. He was tuned in to what was going on around him and even carried on a small conversation. He was also running down the hall and throwing himself into the wall, but a few rounds on the trampoline stopped that. We are very excited tonight. I have an appointment with a nutritionist on Monday. We are a little concerned about Andrew's eating habits and how the diet will affect it. He hasn't been eating well lately.

May 28, 2001

I met with a nutritionist. She recommended acidophilus (anti-yeast) for two weeks to clear out Andrew's intestines. Then, we'll try the gluten-casein-free diet. I've made a list of foods he will eat. It's not quite as limited as I first thought.

Breads/Grains
> White bread with honey or butter (mainly honey), hamburger bun, crescents, biscuits, pancakes with syrup, Cheerios, toast with cinnamon sugar, Kraft macaroni and cheese, white rice, spaghetti, crackers (Wheat Thins, Goldfish, Ritz, Saltines, Cheese-Its, graham, animal, peanut butter/cheese)

Fruit items
> Unsweetened applesauce, bananas

Vegetables
> Mashed potatoes (rarely), French fries

Meats/Poultry
> Chicken nuggets, strips, and fried pieces; hamburger when in spaghetti sauce, pork chops (rarely)

Dairy
> Cheese pizza, cheddar cheese, cheese slices, cherry yogurt without the cherry pieces, chocolate pudding

Sweets
> Ice cream with chocolate syrup (sprinkles), cupcakes and cake (mostly the icing), cookies (sugar, chocolate chip, Oreos, vanilla

wafers), popsicles, donuts, brownies (no nuts), popcorn, M & M's, suckers

Other

Peanut butter & jelly sandwich, regular chips or Pringles

Drinks

Lemonade, milk, fruit punch (rarely), apple juice (rarely), water

[Author's note: In three years, Andrew has only added two foods to this list: corn on the cob and Cheetos. I have heard of other children with ASD who only eat two food items altogether. While this list appears to me to be limited, compared to what the rest of the family eats, it is actually comprehensive for a child with ASD. We will continue to work on getting Andrew to eat other foods. However, because he is healthy, we have focused on tackling other issues before the food issue.]

May 29, 2001

We saw the ENT today. Andrew does not have an ear infection at this time. He didn't cooperate with the hearing test. He didn't want to wear the ear phones and the "box" we have to sit in scared him. The tympanic test showed some fluid behind one ear. The doctor gave us four options: do a month of preventive antibiotics, put tubes back in his ears, put tubes back plus take his adenoids out, or do nothing and watch Andrew for the next two months. We chose to watch him.

June 9, 2001

We just got home from a week in Memphis. We left Jesse there with Mema and Geda. Andrew has done well by himself. He has only occasionally asked where Jesse is and hasn't thrown any fits.

June 11, 2001

We started a summer speech program at UNM today. It is two days a week for two and a half hours a day for six weeks. There are three other autistic children in the program. Andrew cried and clung to me for the first fifteen minutes. The clinician slowly worked with him until he left my lap to play with bubbles. I was able to leave the room after we had been there thirty minutes. He did okay after that. We finished the two weeks of acidophilus. I haven't seen any changes. We've tried the chewable multi-vitamins but Andrew won't take them. He spits them out.

June 13, 2001

UNM speech-language evaluation report:

Andrew is high functioning with good receptive language skills. However, his expressive language skills are diminished. Specifically, he demonstrates difficulty verbally expressing his emotions and with word retrieval. When he cannot recall a word, Andrew quotes movies. In addition, he has sensory issues such as tactile defensiveness and spinning behaviors. His mother reports that new strategies are being implemented to replace the spinning behaviors, such as jumping on a mini-trampoline.

Andrew describes emotional states (happy, sad, hungry, tired) using appropriate adjectives about 20% of the time. He was able to monitor his feelings such as anger or agitation by using a replacement method (stress ball, jumping, punch ball) approximately 10% of the time. He can decrease his rate of speech when cued by the clinician 30% of the time. Andrew can also correctly use a visual schedule while participating in activities at the clinic 20% of the time.

June 18, 2001

I have tried to give Andrew soy milk as part of the casein-free diet. He won't drink it even when it's mixed with regular milk. The diet food (gluten free) is expensive and hard to find. I'm not convinced this will help.

June 20, 2001

Okay, so we've only tried the GFCF diet for nine days, but I'm going crazy! Both Andrew's OT and his preschool teacher (I called her) said it was okay to stop the diet. Andrew is making good progress on his own. The diet is causing me a great deal of stress. There are enough changes going on without adding this. We can always try the diet another time. I'm so glad. I feel relieved … even though a bit guilty.

June 25, 2001

Andrew has been running a fever for four days. He doesn't have an ear infection. The doctor thinks it is a virus. She commented that his behavior in the clinic was much better than usual. He engaged in spontaneous conversation and played actively with toy trains/cars. She saw a "marked improvement in development and speech ability." I had to keep him home from hippotherapy, speech therapy, and swim lessons.

June 29, 2001

At swim lessons, the instructor put pennies in the pool and had the kids try to pick them up, thus practicing putting their heads under the water. Andrew won't put his head under but he did spot a penny. He dragged the penny with his toes over to the stairs where it is shallower and then reached down to pick it up. He didn't have to put his head under the water to get the penny! He was very creative. He has finished the two weeks of lessons. He did well. I don't believe any other parents could see any differences in Andrew. He acted "normal." His tactile defensiveness is almost non-existent when he is in the water.

July 5, 2001

Summary report of Skyline speech-language therapist:

Andrew generally needs time when he first arrives at therapy to organize to the new environment. He has been able to plan and prepare his system for session activities in the past few months when given choices by the clinician about what activity to do first. This allows Andrew to transition his body and thoughts more efficiently. With his "sensory diet" strategy, Andrew has become more aware of what his body needs to be organized and can now use language to express his needs. Andrew's use of "Disney talk" has decreased as he is better able to organize his body and thereby organize his thoughts and language.

Andrew is able to remain on topic and use more complete sentence structure in 80% of all activity-based conversations with the clinician. He is able to respond appropriately for up to five to six turns. Andrew is now able to make eye contact in approximately 30% of his interactions with the clinician. He currently addresses only family members by name and can maintain a conversation for up to five turns approximately 30% of the time.

July 6, 2001

Summary report of Skyline occupational therapist:

Andrew is remarkably more sociable and self-initiates social greetings and appropriate physical contact. He is beginning to experiment with a broader range of food textures and the degree of his resistance to food and previous aversive clothing has ceased or dramatically reduced. With Andrew's increasing presence in conversations and activities around him, his ability to follow directives and make small transitions has dramatically increased.

Andrew is able to stay present and focused in therapeutic activities for periods of up to ten minutes. He requests specific activities, yet is able to wait for periods of up to five minutes with reduced verbal repetition of his request. This progress is observed approximately 60% of the time. Andrew does have periods and/or days when routines have changed or his modulation system is poorly balanced and transitions are very difficult or prolonged. Yet, the dramatic nature of his resistance in these times has reduced and he is able to work through these difficulties with less emotional upset and fear.

July 14, 2001

Jesse tested positive for strep. It was too early to get a positive reading on Andrew, although he has a sore throat and slight fever. Both boys are taking antibiotics.

July 16, 2001

This is the first day of Vacation Bible School (VBS). Andrew got over-stimulated with all the kids, the loud music, and the church looking very different. He didn't know his teachers. He cried and cried. Eventually, one of the teens got him playing ball and I could leave. It was tough. He did okay the last part of the morning. I wish he didn't struggle every time something changes in his world.

July 20, 2001

Andrew did okay the rest of VBS. He didn't participate a lot but he also didn't have many more temper tantrums. We opted not to take him to the Family Night on Thursday since anything in the auditorium seemed to overwhelm him. Uncle Jim and Aunt Kim are here with cousins Michael and Rachel. Andrew is playing well, which is so nice to see.

July 23, 2001

Summary report for UNM Speech-Language Clinic:

Andrew can describe emotional states using appropriate adjectives 70% of the time (up from 20%). [Mom's note: Andrew can describe emotional states using pictures and books but does not recognize them in himself with the exception of hunger and being tired.] Andrew monitored his feelings such as anger or agitation by using a replacement method 50% of the time (up from 10%). He decreased his rate of speech when cued by the clinician 80% of the time (up from 30%). He learned to use a visual schedule correctly 60% of the time (up from 20%).

Andrew attended twelve out of thirteen sessions. He had a lot of energy and was very focused on the activities he considered of high interest. He gradually adapted to the therapy environment and his behavior improved dramatically over the course of the summer. He began to follow the routines of the group sessions, participated in circle time for longer periods of time, and followed directions with minimal resistance. Andrew displayed sympathetic behaviors to another child in the group, trying to comfort him verbally when he was upset. Andrew would attempt to engage both verbally and in play with other members of the group. He is a bright and energetic boy, who will continue to benefit from therapy interventions.

July 24, 2001

There is a graduate assistant helping with the Speech-Language Clinic this summer. She is working on a research project about autism and asked if I would participate. I filled out a questionnaire and was interviewed. I have to admit I surprised myself. She used the word "disability" several times. I finally told her I wasn't comfortable with that word and would appreciate it if she would use the word "disorder" instead. She wondered why it made a difference.

As I thought about it, I realized that to me "disability" sounded so final and so permanent. It was a life-long sentence, and I'm not ready to accept that. I guess I'm still hoping this will all go away. "Disorder" sounds more manageable. I know it's just semantics. It doesn't change Andrew, but it changes the way I deal with it all.

Writing this has showed me how far I have come in the past year. When we received Andrew's diagnosis of ASD on October 10, 2000, I had written that I wanted Andrew to be delayed; that having a "disorder" sounded so final. Today, I have accepted that he has a disorder but not a disability. I wonder what the next year will bring.

July 30, 2001

Today we went to the dentist. Andrew sat back in the chair with sunglasses on to shield his eyes from the light. He let them count his teeth and wipe them with gauze. He felt the electric brush on his finger but wouldn't let them put it in his mouth. That's all he could handle this trip, but it is an improvement from the last time when he wouldn't even let anyone near him.

August 4, 2001

I have been trying to work Super Nu-Thera (SNT) vitamins into Andrew's applesauce. I have heard such great things about these vitamins and how they help kids with autism. But Andrew refuses to eat the applesauce when they are added. The taste of the vitamins is very strong. I haven't seen any improvement, but that could be because I was only able to work up to a third of the recommended dose per day and only for ten days. It just doesn't seem worth the fight at this point. I'd rather he eat the applesauce. We are still doing hand hugs and jumps to help calm him.

[Author's note: Super Nu-Thera is a specially formulated supplement with B-6 and magnesium and other supporting vitamins and minerals. For more information, visit www.kirkmanlabs.com]

August 10, 2001

I had to take Andrew to the Urgent Care Clinic. He has strep throat but no ear infection. He's taking Amoxicillin. I feel like we should have bought stock in an antibiotic supplier. I hate that he has to be on it again, but I'm so relieved that his ears aren't infected. One more infection and we'll have to do the ear tubes again. I'm not crazy about that idea.

August 15, 2001

The OT is thrilled with Andrew's progress. She said two notable things: Whatever we are doing, keep it up because it is working; and second, give him a few years and he won't seem autistic any more. It was positive feedback, but Andrew's "motor" was running high. The rest of the day he was easily frustrated, yelling, and hitting. I wish the "few" years were here!

One More Year of Preschool: Preparing for Kindergarten

❖

(August 2001 – December 2001)

August 23, 2001

I can't believe it's the first day of school already. This year, Andrew is riding the special education bus, which picks him up at the end of our driveway. He jumped onto that bus this morning and didn't look back. I cried. I've been taking him to school for over a year, but there was something about letting him get on the bus and watching them drive off with my baby that got to me. So, this is how other parents feel. I wanted to run after the bus and grab Andrew off it. Jesse has never ridden the bus so I've not experienced this before. Andrew had a great day.

I sent the following "tips" to his teachers. "Andrew talks very fast. Hold your hand out, palm down, and tell him to "slow down." He knows that signal and should repeat what he said but more slowly. You'll still need to get his eye contact. When you have it, point to your ear and say "listen." This is helpful when he is disorganized and not paying attention. Finally, transitions are tough sometimes so we give him one-minute warnings."

The one good thing about school starting is that I can now focus my days on Jesse. I am home schooling him this year so he will get a lot of my attention. And, hopefully, by 3:00 this afternoon he will be ready to have Andrew home again.

August 27, 2001

Note from the school's PT (physical therapist):

We were noticing that Andrew was having a difficult time ring sitting (sitting on floor cross-legged). He has tight hamstrings and low back muscles, which makes him want to sit rounded out. If you could have him try to sit cross-legged with a straight back for brief periods at home, that would help him. Also, he has difficulty holding back extension while he is on his tummy. He could benefit from having tummy time every day. You could have him watch a TV program or put a puzzle together while on his tummy. Maybe he could work these things into his horseback therapy also.

I guess we could work on those things. I have to admit, I'm not worried. I have tight hamstrings, too. It's a family thing.

August 30, 2001

Andrew screamed and cried when it was time to get on the bus today. I ended up driving him to school. He clung to me for a while. I had a very difficult time waking him up this morning. He was still very tired and cranky. The school said he did fine after he was there for about fifteen minutes.

September 7, 2001

Jesse has strep throat again. The pediatrician has prescribed antibiotics for the whole family. Andrew is taking Amoxicillin again.

September 11, 2001

We had an appointment with the eye doctor this morning, so I missed seeing the news "live." Today's attack on the World Trade Center and the Pentagon is a reminder that so many things I think are important really aren't. There are worse tragedies than having a child with special needs. There are worse battles that people face day in and day out. I am very blessed, and I wouldn't trade my family or life. On a side note, the doctor was pleased with Andrew's eyes.

September 19, 2001

Andrew had his therapy with the OT yesterday rather than this morning. He seemed confused. He kept asking if he goes to ride the horse. It's the first time in a long time he hasn't gone on Wednesday morning but I didn't think it would throw him off. We took him to get his birthday pictures taken. He tried to cooperate for about ten minutes and then got overstimulated and couldn't be still. We tried to shop afterward, which was a nightmare. He was singing loudly, yelling, and hitting. It was the worse day he has had in a long time. To make matters worse, Jesse was argumentative, too. I think he was reacting to the stress of Andrew's temper tantrums.

September 25, 2001

Note from school:

Well, eating cafeteria food was a good try. Andrew ate most of the fries. Ms. Gail said, "Andrew, try your chicken nuggets. They're just like McDonald's." Andrew's reply was, "No they're not!" We thought that was pretty funny considering they aren't. They also served peas and an orange, which he would not eat, so it wasn't much of a lunch for him. We gave him crackers and he drank most of his milk.

September 27, 2001

Andrew is five today. He has memorized the response "I'm five" to the specific question of "How old are you?" He holds up one hand when he answers. If I ask him using the word "years," he gets confused. He was excited about all his presents. Happy Birthday, Sweet Boy!

September 29, 2001

Andrew's birthday party with five other kids went well. It's good to see him playing with other kids.

October 9, 2001

Andrew is doing great in the mornings as long as he gets up early enough to get fully awake. Even on the mornings when he is emphatic about not going to school, he runs for the bus when it shows up. He is doing so well and loves school.

October 10, 2001

Andrew slept through the night for four nights in a row but then got up twice Tuesday night. I'm watching his sleep patterns. The insurance company had approved continuing the hippotherapy with the speech-language but had denied OT. We appealed and just got confirmation over the phone that our appeal was successful. He will be able to continue both therapy treatments. However, the insurance company will not be approving any more therapy after the first of the year. We'll cross that bridge when we get there. Truthfully, I'm surprised they've allowed this much. It has been so good for him.

On another subject, Andrew spelled "Jesse" by himself. He undressed and put on his pajamas by himself while I was on the phone.

October 14, 2001

Andrew tasted a Cheeto for the first time and then ate a bowl full. That is the first new food in a long time! What a happy day! Most people wouldn't understand.

While Andrew's communication skills continue to improve, I feel we've hit a wall and we aren't sure where to go from here. We have requested a meeting with the OT and SL from Skyline to get an overall picture of where Andrew's at and what still needs to be worked on. Andrew's annual IEP meeting at school is scheduled for October 24.

We still see a lack of real independent thought. Andrew can tell us what he wants or what he has done, but we don't get any spontaneous expression of feelings or thoughts about things in general. Andrew's communication is very specific, and he uses rote memory. We're thankful for that but still desire more. At school, Andrew can write the numbers 1-25, but at home he writes 1-99 and the whole alphabet.

October 23, 2001

We have been using the brushing on Andrew twice a day for the past month. We do the brush and jumping when he gets dressed and when he put his pajamas on. He loves it. For the past three days, I have pulled his socks up and then turned down the tops. He doesn't fix them! This is a huge tactile victory!

October 24, 2001

Present Levels of Performance reports from annual IEP meeting at school:

1. *Pre-Academic Skills (preschool teacher)*

   Andrew has improved greatly in the area of math and pre-reading and pre-writing skills. He is able to name, identify, and write the numerals 1-30. We will continue to work in the area of one-to-one correspondence. Andrew knows all the letters of the alphabet and is gaining connection as to what they represent. Andrew is ready to recognize words in context and their meaning. He is able to write the letters of the alphabet and his name.

2. *Listening Skills (preschool teacher)*

   Andrew continues to make progress in the area of listening. He is able to complete two- and three-step directions. He also listens to other students' directions made by the teacher and repeats this to the student. He cooperates easily when given instruction most of the time. Andrew rarely has difficulty participating in group activities and attends to tasks appropriately.

3. *Social Awareness (preschool teacher)*

   Andrew has made tremendous gains interacting with peers. He initiates play, makes introductions, and greets peers and adults with enthusiasm. He interacts with adults appropriately unless it is an unfamiliar adult. He may get into a "no" mode with someone he is not comfortable with but has never been physical. It's important for the teacher to validate Andrew's question as soon as possible so that he won't keep repeating it in a parroting sense.

4. *Behavior (preschool teacher)*

   We are no longer seeing pushing or hitting unless another student initiates the same action or behavior. He no longer pushes familiar adults away. Rarely does he not want to share, but when this occurs, time-out still seems to be an effective tool. He may "pout" dramatically but seems to recover in an appropriate amount of time. Andrew continues to improve greatly in this area.

5. *Occupational Therapy*

   Andrew has made great gains (in fine-motor skills). He has shown increased attention to task at hand. He interacts with others. He can cut a piece of paper (on a line) in half by himself. He can write 1-25 and some letters of the alphabet and is able to copy a rectangle and circle. He attempts a triangle. He maintains a tripod grip on pencil. He does have some overflow motions in mouth when cutting. Andrew is showing increasing flexibility with tactile sensations. He loves to touch different clothing textures and can tolerate a variety of textures. He has some intolerance with his right shoe and will take it off at lunch and not put it back on for about two hours. He needs some cues to use both hands in an activity.

6. *Physical Therapy*

   Andrew has made significant progress over the past year (in gross-motor skills). He is participating more in therapy activities. He can play catch with a playground ball and watches with his eyes more intently. He can hop on his left foot four times and his right foot two times. When sitting on the floor, Andrew has difficulty ring or round sitting for very long (five minutes). He has tight hamstrings and low back muscles.

7. *Speech/Language*

   Andrew is currently meeting the goals that were set for him in his last IEP. He is initiating communication with adults without any prompting and maintains that interaction in the context of a story or a shared activity. Andrew comments on the activities that are occurring using novel utterances. Andrew's need areas for language are his processing skills. He needs assistance to begin restating complete ideas using his own words as well as generating ideas when given a picture stimulus.

Andrew understands the concept of "I" and "you." He gets upset when we tease him by saying, "You're a monkey" or "you are a boy." He says, "No. I'm Andrew." We have been trying to teach him when he is angry or sad or happy but have been using the "you are" phrase. He rejects that because he is Andrew! SL recommended saying, "Andrew, when your body feels like that, it's called being angry" (… or sad, or happy, or whatever). It's worth a try!

October 25, 2001

I asked the OT at Skyline why she is the only therapist who is experiencing Andrew the way we do at home (more outbursts and resistance). She thinks it is because at home we make Andrew do things he doesn't want to do. She pushes him during therapy to his threshold and beyond many times. As a result, I feel she has the best understanding of what we face. The other therapists and teachers don't appear to be pushing him nearly as much and, therefore, he is more cooperative and pleasant with them.

Andrew had me read the *Veggicational Book* (*Veggie Tales* 4-in-1 book) to him at bedtime. I had to read all the words! I can't think of any other time he has insisted I read all the words.

October 26, 2001

I mailed in the Waiver Services Registration form to put Andrew on the waiting list for the Developmental Disabilities Waiver (DD Waiver). The DD Waiver can provide him with respite care, therapies, case management and a variety of other services, including Medicaid. However, there is a waiting list of several years. Andrew's name will be added to the list upon receipt of the registration form. Then they will send us a packet of papers to fill out for the formal application.

October 28, 2001

Donald and I talked about Andrew's behavior at home and came up with the following things that we deal with on a consistent basis. We gave it to the OT and SL at Skyline in preparation for our meeting next week.

1. Andrew has to have certain things just right. For example, we ordered red cherry slurpees at Burger King. We didn't know until they gave them to us that the color was black in honor of Halloween. Andrew cried and cried because it wasn't red. He wouldn't taste it to see it was still cherry. He was inconsolable until we found a convenience store and got him a red cherry slurpee. He also has to have his food placed in just the right place on his plate and use the blue spoon when eating from the blue bowl.

2. When he doesn't want you to talk, he won't let you finish your sentence. He says, "No talking. You can't talk." Even if we're trying to tell him something important, he doesn't hear us and won't let us finish. It's the same way with singing. He won't let us sing. He gets very agitated when we sing.

3. Andrew sings very loudly. He has to finish the whole song once started. You can interrupt him to answer a question but he goes right back to where he left off in the song. He fills the silences by quoting movies or singing, but most often we're not allowed to.

4. One good thing is that when Andrew quotes movies, and especially his computer game, he has been substituting our names into the dialogue. He likes it when we help him with the dialogue by taking a speaking part and quoting the game.

5. We sometimes get glimpses of his intelligence that he can't repeat

even a few minutes later. For example, this morning Andrew and I were looking at the pictures on our bedroom wall. We looked at the family picture we took last year in October. He said "that's snow." I said, "Yes, that's snow." He said, "Kevin took that picture." I was floored. Our next-door neighbor, Kevin, did indeed take the picture. It is amazing that Andrew remembered that. When Donald tried to get him to tell him who took the picture not five minutes later, Andrew just repeated his words. Donald said, "Andrew, who took this picture?" Andrew answered, "picture." Donald, "but WHO took the picture?" Andrew, "snow." It's like having an unexpected glimpse though a window and then having the window slam shut and not knowing how to open it again.

6. How Andrew wakes up determines what kind of morning he has. If he wakes up himself and he's happy, he is cooperative and the morning goes smoothly. If he has a hard time waking up, he is demanding, yells a lot, says "no" to everything, and generally can't be pleased by anything.

7. Since we started brushing him twice a day, he hasn't wanted to jump on the trampoline or roll in the blanket. The only other vestibular input he gets (besides the jumping with the brushing) is to mimic his pin-the-tail-on-the-donkey computer game where the donkey spins and dances and then falls down. He loves that.

8. His limited diet continues. He eats mostly pancakes, bananas, bread with honey, spaghetti, applesauce, various crackers, and chips. He drinks milk, lemonade, and apple juice. He drinks water at night.

In the afternoon, we took the boys to the Great American Train Show. Andrew was very excited and loved it. He did well staying with us and didn't yell or argue.

October 29, 2001

Andrew is making great progress. He is ready to learn to read, which is very exciting. He'll have to learn by sight. I'm not sure he'll ever really get the phonics, but who cares? He talks a lot about concrete things – what he did at school – or makes comments about what's going on around him. He is so present in what's going on instead of just on the fringe of life. It's wonderful.

He still doesn't understand abstract ideas. We've been working on teaching him to recognize when he is angry or sad but he hasn't made the connection yet. He says hi to everyone he meets and tells them his name. All his teachers and therapists are thrilled. We are starting to get information about our choices for kindergarten in the fall. He loves to ride the school bus each day.

November 1, 2001
Notes from meeting with OT and SL at Skyline:

1. *Treatment approach – The goal is to get Andrew's system settled down and be able to handle sensory processing. For the OT, the biggest goal is to work on modulation within the sensory process. For every sensation, there is a chemical response. For Andrew, she feels his level of serotonin is too low and the level of nor epinephrine is too high. Andrew's modulation is not working well. His chemicals are out of balance, which leads to unreasonable behavior (e.g., "slurpee madness" – see notes on 10/28/01, # 1).*

2. *"Me in the Picture" is an abstract concept. There is a map in the brain that gives us the ability to make judgments about me and what's in my space. We know where we are, where our hand is, where our stomach is. We reference everything in our world to that map. When we are sick or on medication, everything feels disoriented because our "map" isn't working right. That is how Andrew probably feels much of the time. His attention is focused on small objects. He forgets the last thing he saw or did so he doesn't get the whole picture. It's like learning everything all over again the next time he sees it. His visual sense is his strongest component.*

3. *Nor epinephrine helps maintain attention. If there is too much, you lock into something and can't let go. If there is too little, you can't keep your attention. It is not so much a matter of an attention deficit, but the inside of the body is revved up and there is a lot for the body to do. Nor epinephrine is triggered by new or novel experiences. Much of Andrew's day is a new experience because of little retention of whole picture of experience (see number 2). That is why routines are so important.*

4. *Serotonin sets the level of other chemicals. You don't want it to be too low. Repetition is a grounding tool along with heavy proprioceptive input (jumping, joint compressions). Repetition, rhythm, and music are very important.*

5. *Andrew needs consistent vestibular (movement) and proprioceptive input.*

November 6, 2001

Last night, Andrew had a night terror around 10:30 p.m. He had a difficult time calming down and stopping his crying. He clung hard to Donald. Around 2:30 a.m., he had an accident, wetting his underwear and pajamas pants. Twice during the night, I heard him singing two lines of a song each time, but he did not require my getting up with him.

November 20, 2001

Andrew fell out of a tree from about nine feet up. (We're in Bartlett, Tennessee, at Mema and Geda's house.) He hit his head on a branch on the way down but landed on his side. It scared him badly but didn't seem to hurt him. I think his angel must be working overtime.

November 22, 2001

Andrew was very disorganized this morning: whiny and confused. We were concerned how he would do with so many family members coming over for Thanksgiving dinner. At one point, he sat leaning against me on the stairs. I hugged him close and did hand hugs on his arms and chest. I asked him if his body felt funny. He said, "Yes." I think the closeness, hand hugs, and eating something helped him.

He did wonderful when everyone was here. Several times, he wandered off by himself to sit on the trailer steps and regroup. He also stayed outside nearly the whole time where there weren't nearly as many people or so much noise. I am filled with a sweet amazement at how he is learning what his body feels like and how he can help himself cope. It's slow coming but it is coming.

November 23, 2001

Andrew (and Jesse) spent the night at Aunt Paula's house. It was Andrew's first time away from home, away from us. Aunt Paula says he did great. What an exciting step of independence.

November 25, 2001

We are back from our trip. Andrew was so wound up when we got to the motel last night that we couldn't eat at the restaurant. We had to take our dinner back to the room. He didn't fall asleep until after 10:00 p.m. Motels are very stressful for him because everything is new and different.

December 1, 2001

Andrew has been very disorganized and whiny all day. He is demanding, with a lot of no's and "leave me alone." There has been constant yelling and hitting all day. It's very stressful. He gets a notion in his head about how things are supposed to be and there is no changing his mind.

There is something perplexing that I've noticed. Andrew can spell the word "spelling" but not the word "spell."

[Author's note: Many children with ASD have difficulty with what is called "transference of learning." They may learn a skill or a fact but be unable to transfer or generalize that learning to a different circumstance. For example, a child may be able spell a word for a spelling test but not be able to spell the same word when using it in a sentence. For a long time, Andrew could tell us our "phone" number but not our "telephone" number. To him, the numbers were not related because the words were different. He couldn't grasp the concept that the number was the same!]

December 2, 2001

Donald said a simple prayer at breakfast. Andrew said "Dear God for dinner, not breakfast. God not want pancakes for breakfast." So Donald said, "Dear Jesus, thank You for our breakfast. Is that better?" Andrew said, "Yes." I can't help but feel we are reaching a breaking point with Andrew, and while it's going to be a struggle, he seems just on the verge of having everything come together. He is much more verbal and appropriate and is so aware of what's going on around him. His behavior is pretty erratic right now at home and at school; even at therapy to a degree. Perhaps he is struggling to communicate on a new level and can't quite get there. It is exciting and frustrating all at once.

I attended a meeting where they talked about the Developmental Disabilities Waiver. Apparently, what I mailed in on October 25 was not correct. I will have to go to the office in Santa Fe to fill out the registration form. There is still a five-year waiting list. I'm going to wait and see what happens in the next few months before I begin that process again. We may be looking at some serious changes in the months ahead, including a move across the country.

December 6, 2001

Note from school:

Andrew had an interesting day. He started out getting in trouble with the therapist as we were doing a cut-out activity. He was through with the scissors, but when it was time to put them away, he wouldn't give them up. He was about to poke a few people. We don't know what that was about. We've never encountered that behavior before.

Then before lunch, he got in trouble with me. He washed his hands, but we had asked him before he washed his hands if he needed to use the restroom. He said no, but then ran into the restroom after washing his hands. When he came out, I told him, "Next time, you'll have to wash your hands after you use the restroom." (I knew that making him wash his hands again would upset him, so I just made this comment.) He told me "no" and to leave him alone. Needless to say, he got time-out. The afternoon went much better. It usually does after a time-out. He hasn't had a time-out in so long, but as we both mentioned Tuesday, he's been demanding since Thanksgiving. I just thought you'd like to know how his morning went.

December 10, 2001

Andrew had a night terror last night; the worst in months. He couldn't get off the bed fast enough to cling to me. It took five minutes of deep-pressure hugs to get his body to stop shaking. He finally settled down and got back on his bed. He was partially awake during the whole process – enough to tell me if and when he was ready to get back on his bed. He sure scares me when he does that.

December 11, 2001

Summary report of Skyline's occupational therapist sent to the insurance company:

Andrew continues to progress in the area of fine gross-motor skills. He struggles with fasteners such as buttons, zippers, and snaps. He is now able to put on and take off his shoes and socks. The sock orientation is not always accurate. Andrew is becoming less sensitive to sudden changes but is by no means unaffected by these changes. His levels of resistance to change have reduced, yet his disorganization, and a level of irritability when these changes occur, is very evident.

Andrew has made a significant shift in his ability to communicate some of his needs. He continues to perform in daily activities that indicate an

*increased processing of environmental sensory stimuli. He is becoming much
more engaged in one-to-one and group activities and conversations. Andrew
has been able to identify what sensations help him feel better and has begun to
verbally and physically request specific activities to help him feel better.*

*His parents report that with the exception of the past two weeks, Andrew's
sleep patterns have evened out, and he will go for up to a week without waking up
during the night. It is important to note that while the daily and nightly patterns
have changed (longer periods of contentment and sleep), they are still subject to
periods of discontent and unrest.*

*The area of dietary modifications has been very difficult to treat. Andrew
is very specific about the foods he will tolerate and refuses to eat at all before
eating something he dislikes. His primary food group is carbohydrates. Andrew's dietary needs are a very complex issue. It is felt that there are issues of
tactile discomfort, abnormally strong taste preferences, specific food cravings
related to hormone imbalance, and behavioral resistance to change anything
involved in this area.*

*Andrew has again achieved many new levels of function this reporting
period. It is felt by his family and service providers across all of his environ-
ments that Andrew is on the edge of a major shift in his independent function, communication, and behavioral differences.*

*The greatest concern at this time is the ability to sustain this progress
curve and further solidify his foundation of skills. Andrew remains within
a very important window of early intervention. To stop his therapies at this
time would put Andrew at great risk for loss of function at a critical time in
his development.*

Summary report of Skyline's speech-language therapist sent to the
insurance company:

*Andrew continues to need time when he first arrives to adapt to the new
environment. He has been able to plan and prepare his system for session activities in the past few months when given choices by the clinician about what
activity to do first.*

*When stressed, Andrew uses some rote-learned cartoon dialogue and
songs to organize his body and thereby organize his thoughts and language.
He continues to use songs to maintain self-organization and control overwhelming environmental stimuli. Andrew continues to tolerate up to fifteen
minutes of any given task. He is responding well to cues as time limits for
activities to give him a framework for duration and expectations. [The clinician continues to model] self-talk comments about Andrew's physical and*

emotional state to give him the step between body knowledge/awareness skills [of emotions] and the language used to express that knowledge.

He initiates conversation with the clinician 65% of initial interactions in the session and comments on his environment and activities. He has also related facts about his day to the clinician in short "sound bites." Andrew has been able to tell a story using environmental cues and continue the story theme with original language several times. He is using expanded vocabulary patterns and is developing a more "commanding" form of language as these skills emerge. Andrew is becoming adept at "giving orders" to his parents, the school staff, and his clinicians.

Andrew is consistently maintaining conversations for four to five turns with minimal cues 65% of the time. He is also making more eye contact throughout conversation and is able to address his clinicians and some staff members by name without modeling. He has shown great gains in his ability to make language his own and manipulate it rather than using rote-learned sequences to try to express himself. It is felt that he shows good prognoses for continued improvement. Andrew is not receiving therapy for maintenance reasons. He is actively expanding and maturing in his linguistic skills.

December 23, 2001

Andrew got our scissors and cut the computer mouse cord, Grandma's luggage tag, and a few other things in the study. He was "just playing," he said. I don't think the occupational therapist at the school has to worry about his ability to cut things any more. He did just fine!

December 26, 2001

We have gone swimming at the Holiday Inn Express (Andrew calls it "the fish") three times with Andrew's grandparents and great-grandfather (Gramps). Andrew did very well kicking and clinging. That is his idea of swimming. By the third time, he wanted to go to Gramps and spent a lot of time with him. Andrew still does not put his head under the water and doesn't understand to close his mouth under water.

He is still obsessed with *Thomas the Tank Engine* and *Veggie Tales*. If he doesn't want to do something, he declares that it is dangerous. He does a regular routine of jumps, either on the trampoline or with adult help. He rolls tightly in the blanket and then unrolls. If you displease him, he won't kick or hit you, but he will tap or pat you and then run.

When he gets upset, he runs and wedges his head between the pillows on the sofa with his legs straight, and announces, "I'm stuck." We are supposed to pull him out and repeat the scenario over and over. It becomes a game. He likes to play in the water at the kitchen sink and wash the sink. He is not motivated to dress himself.

December 30, 2001

Andrew had a rough morning. He was really out of sorts. He had his fork leaning against his plate. When I moved his fork in order to put syrup on his pancakes, he nearly lost it. He told me not to move his fork, to never do it again, and to say I was sorry. (Of course, it was more yelling and crying than telling.) I was impressed that, even with an unreasonable response, he was able to communicate what I had done to upset him. Only nine months ago, he would have been screaming and crying but I would probably have never figured out why until he threw the fork across the table. There is progress!

December 31, 2001

Andrew was lying on the couch. I placed a small couch pillow over his stomach and sat on it. He thought it was wonderful and wanted me to do it many times. He enjoyed the proprioceptive input. It was the first time he has allowed me to do deep pressure in that way.

Changes on the Horizon: Preparing to Move

❖

(January 2002 – May 2002)

January 7, 2002

Andrew has had a good break but we haven't kept a routine. Nevertheless I don't think it will take him long to get back into one with school starting. This will be an interesting five months. We've decided to move to Memphis, Tennessee. We've been giving it a lot of consideration. All of Andrew's doctors, teachers, and therapists say the same thing: If we are going to move him, it's best to do all the changes at the same time. It will be a big adjustment for him to go from preschool into kindergarten. We might as well throw the move in at the same time. That way, it's just one big adjustment instead of him getting used to a school and then having to move later on. It makes sense.

It means physical support from Donald's family. They all live there and will be a part of our everyday lives. We haven't had that before. Both extended families are very supportive of us and of Andrew, but while we are living here in New Mexico, there's no one to take the kids for an afternoon or overnight. It will be quite a change but a good one, I'm sure. It will be hard being farther from Mom and Dad but it can't be helped. We'll just have to try to get out to Arizona on a consistent basis. We haven't told the boys yet because we aren't ready for anyone here to know. We'll tell them when it's time to get the house ready to sell in another month or two.

January 9, 2002

What a great dentist appointment. Andrew tried to cooperate with x-rays but gagged on the cardboard when they put it in his mouth. He let them clean his teeth with a rag and count them. It was fantastic!

January 13, 2002

Andrew was sick at his stomach four times Friday night (Saturday morning). Why is it always during the night? So he may not have been feeling well Friday although he showed no indication to us until it happened. He did run a bit of a fever Saturday. We'll see how he does Monday since it usually takes him a week to fully recover from being sick.

January 17, 2002

Note from school:

We (meaning the team) were talking about our students yesterday during our planning time. We were wondering if you could meet with us next Wednesday after horse therapy. We are seeing some "old behaviors" and we'd like to know if you are, too.

Also, we watched a Madeline video for the letter M. It really affected Andrew. As we were gathering for the movie, Andrew ran to the bathroom. I waited and waited. I finally went in and knocked on the door. (He usually never closes the door.) I said, "What's wrong, Andrew?" He told me he didn't want to watch that movie. When I asked, "Why?" he said, "My father is dead" and started crying! (Madeline, if you don't know, is an orphan and in the movie she explains that her father died.) That movie really, really affected him. No more Madeline movies in this classroom.

We thought that Andrew's reaction was so interesting and thought you'd like to know. Andrew had a time-out today. It's been a while since that's happened.

January 23, 2002

I talked with the OT at Skyline. She consulted an outside expert, who says Andrew is in a transitional phase. His brain no longer wants us to "do" things for him. He is ready to do things for himself. He needs help finding socially acceptable ways to get the proprioceptive and vestibular input he needs. I met with the teacher and therapists at his school. They are concerned about "old behaviors" appearing. I told them about my conversation with the OT.

They have also noticed Andrew doing the "stares" again, so we will watch for that. The group did admit that at this point, it appears Andrew would not do well being mainstreamed all day for kindergarten. Perhaps they will put him with the special education teacher and let him go into the regular classroom for certain activities.

January 29, 2002

Andrew has a fever that started Thursday. Today is the fifth day. The cough started Friday or Saturday. Donald has been sick since last Wednesday, and Jesse and I got it Saturday. Andrew's temperature has gotten up to 103.9 degrees. We've all got full-blown flu.

February 1, 2002

Both kids have an elevated temperature again. This is getting old. I've been frustrated all week. I don't like being sick. I really don't like the boys being sick since they are lousy patients. Of course, I'm not "patient" either.

February 4, 2002

Andrew's fever broke Saturday. This morning, he refused to get ready for school and wouldn't go out to the bus. I drove him and took him to his class but had to carry him in. He would not let go of me. He hid his face in my shoulder and cried and cried. I stayed for an hour trying to get him adjusted but he just cried and sat on my lap. I finally broke down in tears and took him home. We are so tired from being sick. I just couldn't take it any more. He did okay once we got home.

February 5, 2002

Note from school:

You sure needed a hug more than Andrew did yesterday! We understood. Today, we got our Andrew back. He got off the bus and came in just fine. He just wasn't ready for me yesterday, telling him what to do. I don't think he was ready for any of us. He's fine today. He ate very well ... considering. He was cooperative and "with-it." He did fall asleep for about ten minutes right before we were to wake up.

February 8, 2002

Note from school:

Andrew was very different today. He was singing a lot and mimicking. He was also talking back and testy. He made strange faces, and I'm not sure if his eyes were crossing on their own or if he was crossing them. Maybe he wanted to see us differently! He was holding himself, but he would tell us he didn't have to go the restroom. He'd say "I don't need to go in there."

He also didn't want to watch a Franklin video. He didn't want to watch a show. Also, he's not drinking anything here at school – nothing. He never drinks milk. Maybe you should send lemonade or something. We ran out of it.

February 13, 2002

Andrew is having his typical tough time getting back into the routine of things, only this time it's compounded by us getting the house ready to sell. He has seen me packing up boxes and taking some pictures down. The house is looking different. I've tried to explain to him what is happening but it's hard to know how much he understands. His behavior has regressed more everywhere but church (unless they aren't telling me). However, his speech has not regressed so it's easier to understand what he wants.

The OT at Skyline told me this morning that she is resigning at the end of this month. She'll have two more sessions with Andrew. The timing is ironic. We (Donald and I) have both been wondering if the hippotherapy is effective any more. I didn't realize she was wondering herself.

There are indications that Andrew has gone about as far as he can for now. I'm not sure about Andrew's working with the speech therapist. Donald and I are discussing several possibilities. We may have the OT come to the house (instead of meeting at Skyline) for a couple of Wednesdays in March to work with him in his own environment. She can help us help Andrew make the transition as smooth as possible. We would, of course, pay her instead of Skyline. She has agreed to go to the school's IEP meeting with me some time around the end of March; I think she would be a great asset for us in giving insight into what would help Andrew in a school setting.

This IEP is very important because we have to take it to the next school system to show what would have been done had we stayed here. I'm trying to get the school to schedule Andrew's testing.

February 20, 2002

I put out twelve cards with words and pictures (boots, coat, cap, dress, plate, fork, chair, crayon, broom, door, bed, and clock). Andrew named them all. Then I asked him, "Which is something we wear?" He picked out the coat. He was a little confused until I used the word "clothes." Then he was able to pick out the other three items we wear. I asked him what we would use to eat. He picked out the plate and fork. He picked the chair for something we sit on and the bed for something we sleep on. The clock confused him. He picked up the broom card and I asked him what it was for. He said, "to clean." He picked up the door card and said it was "to open." It was great. I'm thrilled.

Last night after Andrew's bath, I told him I needed to trim his nails. He said, "No. No nails!" I waited a few minutes, and he eventually came over and presented his feet. As I was trimming his toenails, he asked for a snack. I said he could have one as soon as I finished his nails. He said, "No, Mom. You no do my nails. Those are my toes!" I asked, "Where are your nails?" He said, "Never mind." That's his response whenever he isn't sure what the answer is or when he doesn't want to tell you. "Never mind." We hear it a lot, but it was kind of funny.

February 27, 2002

I think the amazing thing these days is the range of my emotions – actually more than the range is the quickness of how those emotions change. It's easy to feel up and well, and then frustrated, and even apathetic. There usually isn't a known cause. It's just there. I'm sure it's the underlying stress for all of us. Andrew's sleep patterns have been messed up for over a week now. He has a hard time going to sleep but has been getting up at 6:30 a.m.. It's no surprise that he fell asleep at school Monday and Tuesday. I'm not sure what's going on.

March 2002

In preparation for the upcoming meeting with the school, I compiled a written portrait of Andrew including where he is now in terms of behavior and skills. As we look towards helping him adjust to kindergarten, I want them to see the complete picture of who Andrew is and what our dreams for him are.

A Portrait of ASD as Seen in Andrew

Andrew is a loving, sweet boy with a great capacity to learn. In the past year, he has made tremendous improvements in his ability to communicate, which has affected his behavior positively. While he wants to play with peers, Andrew does not understand social cues. He does not realize he is different; therefore, he does not realize he needs to learn different behaviors and skills. The following are characteristics we see in Andrew that are common in children with ASD.

Social/Behavioral Skills

Behavioral issues occur when the environment is overwhelming. Sensory integration dysfunction can hinder a child's ability to fully engage in his or her surroundings. It is important to sort out behaviors that result from inability to deal with his environment and/or sensory integration dysfunction rather than assuming all misbehaviors are noncompliance.

1. *He has a desire to play with others and is learning to play by interacting and taking turns rather than just playing side-by-side. He accomplishes this mostly through games that specifically require taking turns, such as playing sports or matching card games.*

2. *He needs time to transition from one activity to the next. He is improving in this area when given a timed warning. He also needs warnings when his schedule will be significantly changed.*

3. *He lacks making eye contact on a regular basis. Without initial eye contact, Andrew often does not attend to what is being said to him.*

4. *He has difficulty recognizing the emotions others are feeling, as he has difficulty reading nonverbal social cues, such as facial expressions or body language. He does, however, understand a person's tone of voice and responds to either praise or anger in the tone.*

5. *He can be easily excited and unintentionally hurt others when he makes quick, sudden movements without regard for where he is in relationship to the room or others. If he knows he has unintentionally hurt someone, he often responds with empathy or offers "I'm sorry." If he meant to hurt someone, he is not empathetic nor is he sorry. If he is unaware that he caused the person to be hurt, he may laugh at the person's response of pain, thinking he or she meant to be funny.*

6. *He has a low level of tolerance for perceived unmet needs, whether it's for food, a new toy, or an activity he wants to participate in.*

7. *When frustrated, Andrew will yell, hit, or throw things. If he incidentally brushes against something or someone, he will lightly hit whatever touched him. This includes a wall or a stove, or he may chase someone in order to lightly hit him or her.*

8. *He rarely acknowledges the presence of someone he doesn't know. However, in selective play situations such as at McDonald's, he may approach another child and try to get that child to "play" with him.*

9. *He does not understand social rules concerning others' personal space. He may get too close to another person, but not touch them, or may pat a person inappropriately albeit unintentionally.*

10. *He has a limited attention span and difficulty staying on task.*

Sensory Issues

1. *Andrew can easily become overwhelmed by environmental stimuli. This occurs when there are a lot of people, activities, or noises that distract him. He may become aggressive or he may pull away and sing/talk to himself. Often when he is overwhelmed, it is difficult to gain and hold his attention.*

2. *He craves sensory stimulation, but his body does not modulate the input well. He will throw himself onto the floor or run into people in order to get the proprioceptive input his body needs. Sometimes he will spin himself.*

3. *He is sensitive to many taste textures and will only eat a limited variety of foods.*

4. *He is sensitive to maintaining his personal space and does not like light touch. It is painful to him, although he is showing some improvement in this area. He does not tolerate people touching him if the touch is unsolicited.*

Speech/Communication

1. *Andrew uses echolalic speech when he is overstimulated or when he is not able to answer a question. He may also use it when he is simply not paying attention to what is being said to him.*

2. *He quotes movies for stimulation or imaginary play.*

3. *He can understand clear, multi-step directions but may need prompting in between completing the steps.*

4. *He communicates loudly at all times, including singing, quoting movies, or just talking. When prompted, he will lower his voice for a short amount of time.*

5. *He will initiate conversation when he wants something or has something to show you. He does not initiate conversation for the sake of conversation.*

Self-Help Skills

1. He can dress and undress himself when willing, except for zippers and buttons.

2. He is learning to brush his teeth correctly.

3. He can get food out and occasionally wants to help fix it.

Academic Skills

1. He can recognize the letters of the alphabet.

2. He can follow simple directions.

3. He knows most colors and basic shapes.

4. He can play computer games.

5. He is good at matching items.

6. He needs time to retrieve specific answers to questions. Sometimes, he needs cueing to successfully retrieve information.

7. He has difficulty with concentration and staying on task.

8. He learns best by visual stimulation and repetition.

Our goals for Andrew are for him to be a productive, independent adult with a positive self-image, meaningful relationships, and the ability to hold a job he enjoys. Working toward that end, we set four immediate goals to focus on.

1. Our first priority is to see Andrew improve in his ability to gain the sensory stimulation he needs in socially appropriate ways. When his body feels organized, he is more engaged in what is going on around him and is better able to learn.

2. We would like to see Andrew's attention span grow to the point that he can fully participate in group activities and stay on task.

3. We would like Andrew to learn how to express his emotions in constructive ways, particularly his frustration.

4. Andrew's lack of understanding of many unwritten social rules leads to difficulties when he plays with peers. We are concerned about the possibility of name calling, taunting and/or ridicule by other children. We would like Andrew to learn the basic social rules of personal space, "reading" a person's intent, taking turns, and getting along with peers.

March 2, 2002

Andrew yells a lot but generally quiets down when reminded. He gets very upset if we don't do what he wants us to or if we ask him to do something he doesn't want to do. I've noticed, though, that if we don't respond to his verbal tantrums, he will do whatever we've asked. That's nice. He been quoting a lot of movies again but it's different than before. He is play-acting now whereas before it was a means of organizing himself.

As I watch him these days, I find myself very hopeful for his future. Yes, he is still delayed. I know he learns differently, but it is obvious he can learn and is learning. He is a really neat, sweet little boy; that much shines forth. He has been watching *Peter Pan* a lot lately. He uses a wooden ruler as his "sword" in pretending to fight Captain Hook. It is wonderful pretend play.

March 6, 2002

It's been a long day already and it's only 4:15 p.m. We spent an hour and a half at the eye doctor. Andrew's eyes are great. His prescription changed a little but we were going to get new frames for him anyway because he has grown so much in the last year and a half. He should have the new glasses by the end of the month.

The school called today. They are going to do as much formal testing on Andrew as he will cooperate with. They want to do this throughout the school day (and only one person testing per day) instead of bringing him in an extra day. They feel he will be more at ease if it occurs within his regular routine. I will still go and meet with the clinician. There is a test that she and I do together. That will probably happen in a few weeks. Then, we'll have his IEP meeting the first week in April. We are looking forward to having tangible evidence of his progress.

We are getting ready for Andrew's IEP meeting. I learned at the seminar I attended that we have to set the goals before we can decide what the best way to reach those goals is. I know that should be obvious, but it is amazing how often the school set goals for Andrew that sounded good, but we wondered how it fit into the overall picture. Also, we wonder if they are focusing on the highest priority. I'm thinking this next IEP will be vastly different from the previous ones.

We are starting to realize that it's Andrew's social skills that are probably the highest priority right now, even over his communication needs. Things like his lack of eye contact, his inability to "read" facial expressions, and his inappropriate responses to certain situations are interfering with his learning and getting along with people. We are beginning to explore the use of "social stories" to help him understand the correct way to respond in situations. I've heard of it, but he wasn't ready until now to use this particular help.

Judy, the OT from Skyline, came over this morning. She got some wonderful insights into where Andrew is just by watching him around the house. It took a little while, but Andrew did warm up to playing with her. It was great. It was also much easier to discuss things with her without all the distractions at Skyline.

[Author's note: Social Stories™ are a means of helping ASD children and adults learn appropriate responses to social situations. For more information, read *The New Social Story Book* by Carol Gray.]

March 10, 2002

We are trying to teach Andrew his last name. Today coming home from church, Donald said, "You are Andrew Simpson." Andrew said, "No! I no Simpson. I Andrew. Just one!" We'll have to work on this one for a while.

March 11, 2002

Occupational therapy progress summary for Skyline:

Andrew has begun self-initiating the task of dressing himself on a daily basis with no assistance required. He has also begun zipping his coat. He requires assistance with starting the zipper. Andrew continues with his periodic resistance to transitions. There appear to be many layers to Andrew's need to be in charge, making the methods to support him challenging. Some of these layers include inability to fully express himself resulting in frustration, time needed to process the change before being able to act upon it, poor modulation, hence low tolerance for change, and normal childhood resistances.

His parents have reported that Andrew becomes most agitated in the late afternoon and evenings. This is likely related to normal child fatigue, and Andrew reaching his modulation threshold after a build-up of daily stimulation. Andrew is self-initiating periods of running in his backyard along with climbing on his playground equipment. This level of sensory input is far more meaningful and effective to the brain than something more sedentary.

Andrew's potential food allergies and suspect, subclinical metabolic imbalances are felt to be contributing to some of the difficulties Andrew is having with modulation and registration. A consultation with a specialist in nutrition and food allergies is scheduled to occur this month to look further into this area of concern.

Speech and language progress summary for Skyline:

Andrew has demonstrated significant gains when seen for speech language therapy. He has shown great gains in his ability to make language his own and manipulate it rather than using rote-learned sequences to try to express himself. He has recently been able to plan up to three steps ahead when line drawings are made on a white board and he is involved in the planning. Rote-learned dialogue still comprises 50% of all new activity conversation, but he easily transitions out of that when asked specific questions. He often uses this strategy to "jump start" a conversation when he is unsure of how to begin, or he uses the "sound bite" strategy for the same reason when wanting to share information.

Andrew is demonstrating better independently formulated sentence structure 60% of the time. His sentence structure is very precise when "giving orders." He is using proper names and conversational turn taking consistently with 65% accuracy.

March 20, 2002

I had an interesting meeting with Judy (OT) today. She brought another therapy ball since ours was sliced and irreparable. Andrew loves it. We spent some time talking about what has been happening with Andrew lately.

Andrew has not slept through the night seven out of the last eight nights. On Sunday, he was throwing toys at church and tried to hit the teacher before they called Donald in to calm him down. The rest of the morning went fine. His progress report from school shows many areas where he went from "satisfactory" to "needs improvement." Much of it had to do with paying attention, staying on task, and expressing his emotions appropriately. We talked about how he has regressed behaviorally since Thanksgiving, so it can't be just that he's bored at school.

Judy keeps coming back to the nutritional aspect. She says that as she has watched us here at the house and talked with me, she feels Andrew is getting enough sensory input. The problem is that it isn't lasting as long as it should. She feels there has to be something else going on and that it is probably in line with the nutrition and what he may be allergic to.

She has referred us to a doctor in Santa Fe who does "applied kinesiology." He does muscle testing as an aid to diagnosing allergies and what isn't working right within the body. Judy says he is one of the best in this area. Of course, it isn't "western medicine," but Donald and I talked about it and we are willing to see what this guy says. He does have working knowledge of autism and related medical circumstances. We have an appointment with him a week from Friday (29th) for a consultation. If I understand correctly, he should be able to tell us a lot. Judy is going to the appointment with us if her schedule will allow. I haven't heard back from her yet.

I know in my heart that the nutrition is going to play a part with Andrew's progress. I can't make any big changes for months – not with all the other transitions. But it is possible to make smaller ones towards a bigger goal. Jesse and Andrew are really going at it today. It makes me glad we haven't moved yet. Andrew will be in school tomorrow.

[Author's note: I have recently learned that "applied kinesiology" is a questionable practice at best and should be considered only after thorough research and careful deliberation. Our family was unsatisfied with the experience, as noted in the following journal entries.]

March 23, 2002

I don't know what to do with Andrew. Last night (in the middle of the night) I was so angry I wanted to kick the washing machine. It's been a long time since I've felt this way. At the slightest "no," he yells, hits, kicks, and scratches. He is unreasonable and terribly demanding. He is loud and won't obey, and the sleep problems continue. Donald and I lost track of how many times we got up with him last night. Yet, Andrew was up at the usual time this morning. He talks to us using movie talk, especially when he is angry. We can't get him to stop and that gets us even more frustrated than we already are. Spring break is next week so he'll be home all day. I need to make a plan.

March 24, 2002

At church, a girl asked Andrew when his birthday is. He said, "September." We've been telling him that for the past week. He wants a *Thomas* toy, and we keep telling him "maybe for your birthday in September."

March 28, 2002

We had our last visit to the ENT today. Andrew hasn't had one ear infection since last summer. Praise God! Everything looked fine. We are beginning the final round with all the doctors and specialists in preparation for our move.

March 29, 2002

We had a good trip to the doctor in Santa Fe. I was extremely grateful that Jesse wasn't there and that Judy was. The doctor's office was not kid-friendly. There were multitudes of vials and bottles. Andrew had a hard time leaving them alone. The room was also small. Jesse would have been miserable not being able to explore things.

Judy met us at the office. She was a tremendous help, especially towards the end. She took Andrew outside to run around while I finished talking to the doctor. There's no way I could have concentrated if I had had to worry about what Andrew was getting into. Andrew did well. He was fairly cooperative and not only acknowledged the doctor's presence, but didn't throw a fit about the doctor touching him. He wasn't comfortable with it, but didn't throw a fit.

The results are that Andrew is allergic to bananas and casein (dairy products). The good news is that gluten doesn't appear to bother him. He is also deficient in calcium, zinc, folic acid, and B12. The doctor was able to give us liquid forms of the vitamins and minerals except the B12. I'll try to find that tomorrow at the health food store. Our plan of action is to get rid of the casein in the house as soon as possible. I still have all my notes from the diet trial of last summer. When I go to the health food store in the morning, I'll get most of the items replaced. Andrew doesn't know it but he had his last dish of real ice cream tonight. We will stop offering milk. I will cook with soy milk. We are going to try to keep the 2% for the rest of us. If Andrew starts asking for milk, though, it will have to go. He hasn't wanted it lately so I hope we're okay there. The bananas are already out of here. I was amazed when that one came up, but Andrew hasn't wanted a lot of those lately either.

We started giving the vitamins tonight. They hide real well in apple juice and applesauce and even in water. I'm excited about that. We've had a hard time finding vitamins he would take. It looks like these will work. As soon as we get rid of the casein completely, it should take about three weeks for Andrew to get the stored-up casein out of his body.

The doctor said we should notice a gradual improvement in his behavior. Andrew will begin to feel better and his body will function better. I asked the doctor how these foods were affecting him. He said, "It really messes his body up." Anyway, we should see better moods, less resistance, better attention span – all the things you would expect once a person who has been under the weather gets to feeling better. If we are still here in a month, I may take him back for a follow-up. There needs to be enough time to let the casein get out of his body. Then the doctor can do some more tests to "see if anything needs tweaking." He said Andrew has some yeast in his intestines but that is a secondary problem to the reaction to casein. He said we don't have to address that at this time. It may clear up on this diet.

And finally, we have to get rid of the hydrogenated fats (which is most of the food in our pantry). It's not healthy for any of us, but especially not Andrew. We will begin to weed those out but I'm not going to stress over that at this time. The casein is our first priority. We were told specifically that McDonald's French fries were an absolute no-no. I'm still in mourning.

I feel pretty excited about the findings. Taking casein out of our diet at home won't be easy but it will be much better than if we had to worry about the gluten, too. This will be hard but we're up to the task. I think the biggest challenge will be making Jesse's birthday cake with no milk protein in it. I hope they'll have one at the store tomorrow.

April 6, 2002

Letter I delivered to teachers at church:

This letter is to inform you that Andrew has been tested for various food allergies. We have discovered that he is allergic to bananas and casein. Casein is a milk protein that is found not only in dairy products, but in a variety of other foods as well. He has been on a casein-free diet for a week and appears to be doing well. The following are snacks known to be given during Sunday morning services that Andrew CANNOT have: Goldfish, cheese crackers, Cheez-Its, and animal crackers. He CAN have Ritz crackers, graham crackers, and Saltines. We will provide a bag of crackers for Andrew that will be in his cubby to be given to him during snack time.

If you have questions about any food items given during your class, please ask me and I will check the ingredients. He can have lemonade and apple juice. Donald and I appreciate all that each of you has done to help Andrew enjoy being at church. He continues to make progress, and we are excited about the improvements this diet should produce. Again, if you have any questions, please don't hesitate to ask.

April 7, 2002

We went roller-skating for Jesse's birthday. At first, Andrew said he would just watch. When we got there, he wanted to skate, but the loud music and flashing lights combined with the skates was too much for him. Fortunately, he was happy to play air hockey. We had an organic cake with organic frosting. The kids didn't know and loved it. I'm glad.

Andrew's been on the diet for a week. He seems to be doing fine. It may be wishful thinking, but he seems to be more alert and is using more conversational-style language. This morning, he told me he wanted Cheerios but couldn't find the stool to reach them. He sang the *Veggie Tales* song *with* the video. I hope it's the diet and vitamins helping. His Sunday School teachers said he did very well today. It's good.

April 10, 2002

What a day. Andrew was particularly trying today. I lost count of how many times he hit and kicked me plus the yelling and scratching. I finally had enough. I haven't cried that hard in a while. I know the diet and vitamins are helping. I know Andrew is improving. It's hard not to let my expectations get too high. I have to keep reminding myself that this isn't a cure and it's not an overnight success. Andrew will be Andrew. I lost sight of that today.

April 13, 2002

Andrew walked into the bathroom, stood over the toilet, and threw up three times this morning. He did this on his own. He is a little pale and listless but doesn't have a fever.

April 15, 2002

School's multidisciplinary evaluation report:

In looking back to Andrew's behavior and interaction during the previous testing session, Andrew has made significant gains in his ability to participate in activities and follow instructions. He responded positively to the encouragement offered when transitioning from one task to another.

Andrew's performance on the K-ABC on the test day indicates his mental processing composite falls within the Average range, ranking him at the 27th *percentile. The chances are 90 out of 100 that his mental processing composite is somewhere in the range of 85 to 97. There is a significant 34-point discrepancy between his Sequential Processing score of 74 in the Well Below Average range and his Simultaneous Processing score of 108 in the Average range. <u>These results suggest that Andrew's preferred learning style/cognitive approach to problem solving is one that involves processing information in a holistic manner.</u>*

The Woodcock-Johnson Revised Skill Cluster subtests were administered to measure pre-academic skills. Pre-reading skills fall at K.7 grade level; pre-math skills at K.0 (16%) grade level; and pre-writing skills at K.0 (22%) grade level.

The Vineland is an adaptive behavior rating scale that is based on parent interview. It covers the domains of Communication, Daily Living Skills, Socialization, and Motor Skills. The initial Vineland was taken when Andrew was three years, one month old. The current Vineland was completed when Andrew was five years, six months old.

- *Overall Communication skills went from 1-11 age level to 3-4 level, with significant gains in receptive and written language. Andrew now says at least 100 recognizable words and speaks in full sentences. He uses "a" and "the." He understands instructions presented in "if" or "then" forms, and asks "wh" questions.*

- *Daily Living Skills went from 2-4 age level to 3-2 age level. He can put shoes on the correct feet, can dress himself, and put his clean clothes away. He assists in food preparation.*

- *Socialization Skills went from 3-0 age level to 3-2 age level. Andrew seems to engage and interact more with the people around him. He apologizes for unintentional mistakes.*

- *Motor Skills went from 2-5 age level to 3-10 age level with significant gains in fine-motor skills. Andrew is able to cut across a paper, draw more than one recognizable form, and unlock key locks.*

Speech-language evaluation report:

During the language evaluation, Andrew was given a combination of standardized and nonstandardized tests to determine his overall language function. This testing revealed strengths in Andrew's ability to label pictured items and determine the meaning of sentences of increasing length and complexity when provided with visual interpretations.

Andrew was able to demonstrate his ability to follow oral directions in order to reveal his knowledge of basic language concepts related to position, quantity, and attributes of objects. Andrew's performance during language sampling tasks such as story generation demonstrates that he is acquiring and incorporating language through interactions with his environment when the information is provided verbally and visually.

While Andrew is gathering information through environmental input, he is not organizing it well enough to communicate thoughts and ideas without placing the burden on his communicative partner to interpret and produce meaning when the ideas are out of context. Andrew's struggle in the area of language processing, the ability to organize external input, make a meaningful match with his own information store, and retrieve it for practical use will impact his academic success and demonstrates a need for extra services.

Occupational therapy reevaluation:
Andrew's overall Fine-Motor Quotient from the PDMS-2 fell slightly Below Average (it should be noted that a ceiling level was not reached). He has made significant gains in all areas. Over the past three years, he has come from not interacting with others to being able to play with peers in adult-directed games. Andrew is learning how to interact with his environment and become more flexible in thought and risk taking. This process is working in partnership with his sensory/tactile system, which is refining itself. Activities need to be of a short duration, approximately 15-20 minutes, and provide him with multi-sensory information in a nonthreatening approach.

Physical therapy evaluation:
Andrew has made tremendous gains in the area of gross-motor skills in the past few years. He went basically from being untestable with moderate delays in gross-motor skills observed to being able to be given standardized measures. He is now performing in the average range in the area of gross-motor skills but he has continued postural concerns due to low muscle tone in his trunk and muscle tightness in his proximal extremities. He has better posture when he is actively engaged in an activity. Sitting comfortably on the floor, sitting in a chair, and standing in good alignment are all skills necessary at school for optimum learning to take place in a kindergarten environment.

My thoughts on all the evaluations:
For next year, it was decided that Andrew would have his homeroom with the special education teacher (all academics) and would be

pulled out to join the general education kindergarten class for things such as library, music, computer and P.E. As the year progresses, he will join the general education class more and more as he is able. He will continue getting speech therapy and occupational therapy but will be dropping the physical therapy as he is now within the average range.

All of the therapists were thrilled with how well he is doing (that is, for Andrew). Donald and I are feeling many things tonight. Yes, we are thrilled with how well he is doing, the progress he has made, and the fact that he could even cooperate with the testing. We are also saddened at how delayed he still is in certain areas. I know we have to just keep at it, working hard and getting him the help he needs. I feel confident that he will be able to one day fully compensate for his limitations, but for tonight, we hurt for our little boy.

April 23, 2002

Andrew was up for two hours in the wee hours of Saturday morning. Then, he threw up (fortunately he had a bowl). After that he slept for six hours but ran a low-grade fever, so I kept him home from church Sunday. Monday morning he was so tired and really out of it. He wasn't cooperating so he missed the bus. I had to take him. He cooperated after I bribed him with a new train. He didn't want me to come into the school ("You stay in the van").

What was interesting to me was that, as we entered the building and rounded the corner, Andrew suddenly stopped. There were at least twenty adults and kids milling around the hallway outside the office. Andrew watched them for about five seconds and then, without looking, reached up his hand for me to hold. Suddenly I was his friend. He held my hand through the crowd and all the way to his classroom. Once there, he walked over to circle time to join the class and never looked back. His first words off the bus in the afternoon were, "Mom, did you find Oliver?" (The train I promised). He has a good memory.

April 24, 2002

It seems I only write when I'm upset. I wonder why that is. Perhaps it's because that's when I need the most help sorting through all the emotions. I'm so frustrated. I'm tired and almost all cried out. I needed space but Andrew wouldn't (couldn't) leave. I needed quiet and he just kept yelling movie lines at me – even from behind the door. I could still hear him. He can't clear out like Jesse can. That makes me angry.

April 25, 2002

I bought a chair wedge for Andrew to sit on to help with his posture. It's the same kind he uses at school. He loves it. I also got a clown punching bag (the kind that pops back up). Jesse loves it. Andrew is still trying to figure out how it works. Also, Andrew got a short, buzz haircut. Tonight, he got his comb out and asked me to comb his hair. He liked it and said it felt good.

April 26, 2002

This morning, Andrew hit at the clown punching bag when he had his back against it. He was surprised when it popped back up and hit him in the rear end! The look on Andrew's face was so funny. He whirled around to see who had hit him. Later in the afternoon, Jesse got mad and threw the punching bag against the closet door and broke it.

April 29, 2002

I'm stumped. Andrew was sick again this morning. He slept well last night but got up this morning with diarrhea (not unusual with all the apple juice he drinks). Then he threw up twice within thirty minutes. His temperature went up to 99.4. He did well throughout the day but threw up again around 3:30 p.m. This is three times in three weeks. I can't figure out what's going on. Is it related to the diet? The vitamins? A weak stomach? It's very puzzling. I already have an appointment set up with the Santa Fe doctor for Wednesday. Maybe he'll have some answers.

May 1, 2002

We went to the doctor in Santa Fe. Andrew did very well. It was rather interesting but my skeptical side is showing. I'm just not sure how the doctor can get the information he claims he does the way he does. I asked him about Andrew getting sick once a week for the last three weeks. He said it could be several things.

Andrew may be reacting to something he is eating, now that the casein is out of the way. We are to log what he eats before he gets sick to see if there is a pattern. He also has some bacteria in his stomach/intestines. The doctor said that Andrew may have gotten a hold of something bad enough to cause a little stomach bug but that the infection hasn't cleared his system. When enough bacteria builds up, it makes him vomit. That brings the bacteria level back down and the cycle continues. The doctor gave us something to give to Andrew for two weeks to clear the bacteria out. I'll be interested to see if Andrew gets sick again in five days or if it's over.

The doctor also checked Andrew for residue of the MMR vaccination (measles-mumps-rubella) he received at fifteen months. He said he found some, especially around his liver. So he did some "tweaking" (chiropractor talk) at all the acupuncture sites. Andrew thought he was tickling him. Anyway, supposedly Andrew didn't react to the MMR after the doctor was done. The doctor said it was like reprogramming the body. I confess I'm skeptical. I've never heard of this. I guess the proof will be if Andrew continues to show improvement as he "should."

One other thing is that Andrew reacted a little to potatoes. So, the doctor wants us to cut out potatoes for two weeks and see how he does. At first I thought, cut out French fries and mashed potatoes? Okay, that's not bad. When I got to the van, though, it occurred to me – that means chips, too! Andrew will not like that one bit! We're staying on the regime of the vitamins; no new ones were added, so that's good.

Other Andrew-related news: I found a summer speech-language camp through the University of Memphis Speech and Hearing Clinic. It's a similar program to what Andrew did last summer. It is three days a week, two hours a day for five weeks. With one holiday, that is a total of fourteen days. It's for kids age five to ten, mostly autistic but some with just language disorders.

One of the neat things is that they have two or three peer helpers in the camp. They prefer a sibling or near relative to the children in the camp. They are very interested in letting Jesse be a part of it. I'm thrilled because they won't let me "hang out" at the camp. They make the parents say good-bye at the door. We can observe through a one-way mirror but we can't participate with the kids. They will let me bring Andrew to the clinic to meet the therapists and see the room a couple of times before the camp starts. That will make it much easier for him to separate once the camp starts. Plus if Jesse is with him, I think he will be just fine. It's pretty expensive but it will be the only therapy we'll provide for the summer.

We're going to have Judy (OT) continue to come over to the house once a week for this month so that June will be the only time Andrew won't be in a therapy. We don't want to go longer than four weeks without any therapies.

May 2, 2002

Andrew had one bout of diarrhea first thing this morning; then one episode of vomiting. There wasn't anything in his stomach so it wasn't much. But unlike Monday, he ate toast and drank apple juice with gusto. He had no elevated temperature and was running around – even jumping off our filing cabinet. After watching him for an hour, I took him to school, explained the situation to Mrs. B., and he did fine.

I'm still stumped by what is making Andrew sick to his stomach once every week or so. I did let him eat French fries yesterday for lunch. It seems strange that he would be reacting to potatoes when he eats chips like crazy but doesn't get sick every day. There's only one way to find out. Potatoes are out. The chips are hidden for two weeks. We'll see if he gets sick again. In two weeks, we'll give him some potatoes and see how he reacts. I sure hope it's a bacterial infection and not the potatoes. He loves chips. He also loves French fries.

May 4, 2002

Andrew has done very well the past few days. He has yelled a lot today when he didn't get exactly what he wanted, when he wanted it. But overall, he has been more alert, more "present," and more talkative. He has asked for white donuts and bananas today – a first since we started the diet. Tomorrow, we are going to let him eat casein at the going-away party. It will be the first time since March 29. I'll be watching him like a hawk tomorrow night, Monday, and Tuesday to notice any changes. He won't get a lot of casein, but there will be cookies and brownies at the party.

May 7, 2002

Andrew had casein on Sunday afternoon in the form of one brownie, five sugar cookies, and a half a peanut butter cookie. He slept okay but got up at 6:15 Monday morning. He did well at school but once he got home, he argued about nearly everything when he didn't get exactly what he wanted. He didn't go to sleep until after 10 p.m.

He did fine this morning (I had to wake him up at 7:30). Again, this afternoon, he has no tolerance for unfulfilled expectations. He wanted me to get two Larry-Boys today. I got his cloth Larry-Boy out of storage. He is very upset because it isn't bigger. He won't let me take the small one away but he yelled and complained for several minutes because it wasn't the right one. He is very excited about having cake for Daddy's birthday. I found some organic chocolate pudding he loves and some wheat hamburger buns he will eat.

May 9, 2002

I feel, well, cheated almost – at least on Andrew's behalf. His class is doing a field trip on Monday to McDonald's. I'll have to keep him home. He can't have the chicken nuggets (casein) and now he can't have the French fries since he is still off potatoes. What is more frustrating is that he doesn't understand why he can't have these foods. I told him he can't have bananas because they make his body feel funny. He got mad and yelled that they did not make his body feel funny. It's so hard. I can only pray that it was the bacterial infection that made him sick and not potatoes. I can't imagine never taking him to McDonald's again. It's been a week since he's been sick.

On another note: I feel like I'm being pulled in two. In one ear, the beautiful music of *Jesus, Holy and Anointed* tugs at my heart and soul. I want to lose myself in the music and words and let my spirit rest and soar. I cling to Him. In the other ear is Andrew yelling from his bed. "Mom, you're not my best friend." "I don't need you any more." "I'm not going to sleep." "You had your choice." "I don't want it like that." It breaks my heart, and it makes me cry.

I'm tired of being yelled at. I'm tired of Andrew and Jesse getting into it every night at bedtime. I'm just tired. What am I going to do this summer? Andrew's last day of school is next Friday and he'll also be home this Monday. The days get so long with him home all day with his constant demands and yelling when they aren't met to his satisfaction and in his time. I dread the summer almost as much as I dread this move. It's easy to say that Andrew will be an independent, fully functioning adult some day. Some day isn't today. For today, I'm having trouble seeing past the next few months.

May 10, 2002

Andrew woke up at midnight and 2:00 a.m. not feeling well. He threw up at 2:30, 3:30, and 6:00 a.m. His temp. went up to 99.7 and stayed there half of the day. He has diarrhea and is not very active. He isn't hungry and only wants popsicles. He threw up again at 6:30 p.m. He wants to sleep on the floor.

I made an appointment to talk to his pediatrician on Monday. We are stopping all vitamins and minerals until that appointment but are continuing the silver. I talked with the nurse at the Santa Fe doctor's office. She said that the exact dosage for the vitamins and minerals is not in Andrew's file (# of squirts given, but not # of milligrams). She suggested diluting his apple juice (acid upsets stomach lining). I am to look up colloidal silver on the Internet because ionic silver is too new to find any published information on. Then I talked with Judy. She agrees we need to look at the vitamins as the cause for Andrew's sickness and suggested giving half a dosage or cut all vitamins and reintroduce one at a time.

May 11, 2002

Andrew woke up with diarrhea at 3:30 a.m. and stayed awake until 5 a.m. He is grouchy today. He felt better as the day progressed, as evidenced by his improved energy and behavior.

May 14, 2002

Yesterday, I took Andrew to the pediatrician and gave her the history of his sickness and the vitamins/minerals taken. She looked up folic acid and B12. He is getting mega doses of both, either of which can cause nausea and vomiting. We were not able to determine the exact dosage of calcium and zinc being taken. I feel foolish when I realize I have blindly followed this doctor to the point that I didn't even know how much vitamins I've been giving Andrew. "5 squirts." What does that really mean? I called the vitamin company and they told me. He's okay with the calcium and zinc. The pediatrician agrees that it is probably the B12 or folic acid that is causing the problem. We've decided not to give Andrew any more vitamins for two weeks to see if he still gets sick. If not, we'll know.

I showed her the list of vitamins and minerals that are in the Super Nu-Thera formula we tried late last summer. We agreed that if I supplement it with calcium, the formula is a much more reasonable combination. We will probably try that formula again.

I am going to cancel our last appointment with the Santa Fe doctor. I'm just not sure I buy into all of what he is doing. We've had Andrew off the potatoes and will reintroduce them this Sunday. I know tomatoes also may be a trigger to check for later. There is no way to really know until we eliminate a food for a while and then reintroduce it.

This move is a great opportunity to clean out the pantry, refrigerator, and freezer. When we get settled in a new home, it's a chance to only bring good things into the house.

This nutritional aspect sure is complex but I'm doing a lot of reading and studying. We can all eat a lot better. I need to do better with Andrew's "sensory diet." He plays a lot outside and inside with Jesse, which is good. He also hasn't felt very well at least half the time the past month. He finishes school this Friday and then he's home all summer. It makes the days seem long and stressful. I'm so glad we're moving closer to help.

The school called me at 2:15 to pick up Andrew. The class had gone to the zoo. After lunch, he had bad diarrhea, complained of a stomachache, and was no longer interested in looking at the animals. He lay down on the bus on the way back to the school. When I picked him up, he looked fine and said his stomach felt better. He did have a temperature of 99.3 when we got home. He has eaten and played well. He drank a lot of lemonade, something he hasn't wanted for several weeks.

May 15, 2002

Andrew had a rough night between 12 a.m. and 5 a.m. He threw up at 5 a.m. and still has diarrhea. Judy came at 9 a.m. and noticed how out of it he was. She called it "mindblindness," where he can only see his point of view and no one else's. That's why he reacts so strongly when we don't agree with him.

I called the pediatrician. She had me get three stool samples. (That was extremely gross. Was that really in the fine print when I signed up for this parenting thing?) We should get the test results back on Monday. In the meantime, Andrew doesn't feel well and is behaving like a royal pain. It's hard to remain patient.

[Author's note: Mindblindness is described as an inability to understand what is in the mind of another person. It is not necessarily caused by an inability to imagine what others are thinking of feeling; rather, it is often due to not being able to gather enough information (e.g., read body language and other types of nonverbal communication) to accurately determine the thoughts and feelings of others. For some people, such as those on the autism spectrum, the difficulty lies in understanding that others have different thoughts or beliefs than they themselves do. These concepts are also known as theory of mind.]

May 16, 2002

Andrew has been a real pill the last week and a half. His tolerance level has been at zero. I know some of it is because he doesn't feel well half the time, but his attention span has been low as well. Perhaps he is picking up on our rising stress levels. We are trying to remain calm, but he can pick up on internal stress even if the outside is doing fine. Judy understood and didn't blame me for canceling the appointment with the Santa Fe doctor, but she said she would call him and ask him what he thought was going on. Andrew's concrete language is improving but not the abstract.

The other thing we've noticed lately is that, while he can feel empathy if someone is hurt, Andrew does not seem to understand that other people have wants and feelings that are different from his. If he wants to play baseball and we say that we don't want to, he just doesn't get it. He wants to, so we are supposed to want to.

In getting ready for the move, I'm trying to pack a box or two here and there, waiting for the big push next weekend. Andrew tried to help me yesterday. I had a box of board games plus some miscellaneous toys in a box. He kept putting some of his toys in the box that I wanted to leave out. I'd leave the room for something and he'd put the toys in. I'd come back in the room and take them out of the box. I'd leave again and he'd put them back in again. We must have done this three times. He knows he wants to take all his stuff but is having a hard time with "not yet."

May 19, 2002

Andrew has had only had two cups of apple juice since Wednesday. Now all he wants to drink is lemonade. His diarrhea is gone. He was very explosive before church. He has been screaming the last week or so. Not yelling – screaming. He's like a time bomb always ready to go off. There's no warm-up either. It's always when we don't do or say exactly what he wants, when he wants, and how he wants.

We had Jesse's good-bye party with his friends this afternoon. Andrew hasn't had any potatoes in two and a half weeks. Today, he's had several bowls. We're watching him closely for any adverse reaction. He played baseball with the other kids and did the piñata but that's it. The rest of the time, he was inside by himself. When the candy spilled out of the piñata, he only picked up the suckers.

May 22, 2002

The pediatrician finally called after dinner with the lab results – three days late. Anyway, all the tests came back negative. There were no infections or bleeding. Andrew's fine. We both concluded that it was the vitamins that have been making him sick. He seems to be doing a lot better. He has only wanted lemonade lately so the lack of apple juice has cleared up his diarrhea. He is feeling better – no stomachaches. We have to get past tomorrow and Friday to know if he has finally kicked the once-a-week sickness. Our plan is to start him back on a much lower dosage of vitamins after we get to Memphis if he doesn't get sick between now and then.

His behavior has improved over the past few days. He is back to yelling (not screaming) and has a little tolerance (10% as opposed to 0%). I think the more relaxed schedule of not being in school helps as well as getting off the vitamins. He even showed some real pretend play this past weekend. He has been wearing his Superman pajamas. The other night, he told me to say good night to Superman. I said, "Good night, Superman!" He said, "Good night!" Then, this morning, Donald called him Andrew. He said, "I'm not Andrew. I'm Superman!" It's the first time he has been anyone other than Andrew. We love it.

Tonight, he did something funny and I said, "You're such a goober." He responded, "Yeah, I am." Oh, he hasn't shown any adverse affects to eating potatoes again. We are trying to limit how much he has, though, so we don't push it.

May 26, 2002

Yesterday, Andrew had three slices of cheese pizza at a party. He had a stomachache around 1:15 a.m. but then slept fine. He is out of sorts this morning: low tolerance, yelling, limited attention span. He also has red cheeks.

He's been a big help in packing the boxes. Sometimes, he adds things I'm not ready for. At other times, he takes everything out of a box I'd packed to see what I put in it. Overall, though, it is good for him to be involved because he is realizing everything we have is going with us.

Adjustments:
New Address, New Town

❖

(June 1, 2002 – August 9, 2002)

June 1, 2002

While moving, our truck broke down outside Amarillo, Texas, so we've spent two unscheduled nights at a motel. Andrew has done very well. He slept in a queen bed by himself and didn't fall out. (Uncle Steve Lipford is helping us move. Jesse slept in another room with him, which has been a huge help.) Andrew has taken this delay well. We still have a motel room tonight before reaching Memphis tomorrow. Yesterday we went to Chuck-E-Cheese. Andrew had one slice of cheese pizza, and we haven't seen any negative reaction. He also hasn't gotten sick since the vitamins cleared his system.

June 4, 2002

The boys are doing well and did fantastic through the whole Amarillo "vacation." By the second night, Andrew was calling the motel room our "new house." I sent a letter of introduction to the Department of Special Education for Shelby County Schools along with the paperwork to get an IEP for Andrew in the works.

June 11, 2002

Note from Judy (OT):

I wanted to let you know that I had a good visit with the Santa Fe doctor. I didn't call you because it wasn't earth-shattering and I didn't want to interrupt packing progress. He talked for some time during my appointment about Andrew's illness. He stated that if his body was getting too many vitamins he would pee them out. He then became suspect of stomach bacteria. He said that

99

bacteria feed on the folic acid and that could have been creating the vomiting and diarrhea.

He said that the dosages given to Andrew were based on what his body needed at the time and that he was mindful of you returning in two weeks, anticipating that the dosage would need to be adjusted then. He was sorry he didn't get an opportunity to visit with you. He said he would have been happy to problem solve with you over the phone and make adjustments. He sympathized with your alarm at the dosages. He hoped that you would continue with this approach as he felt Andrew was responding well.

So that was his response. I know that you will proceed with what feels safest and best for Andrew as you always have.

June 13, 2002

Andrew has been doing well up to a few days ago. Lately, he's been a real pill, but we've played with his diet some. We have decided that McDonald's chicken nuggets are definitely out. He has stopped eating the foods that he couldn't get enough of the past month – spaghetti and pancakes. Now, he wants honey sandwiches. I think once we get into our own house, things will get better. We don't have much of a routine while living with Donald's parents, which is strange when I think about how we don't have much to do. You'd think it would be easy to set a routine but it's really not.

We put an offer on a house this afternoon. We are very excited about it and hope it works out. We should hear something tomorrow. I know the boys will love it and it's within a bicycle ride of their school. We should also hear tomorrow about the couple trying to buy our house – whether they can afford it or not. It sounded like it should go through.

Everyone here is very impressed with how well Andrew is talking and how well they can understand what he is saying. Most of them haven't seen him since Thanksgiving. We get to go swimming about twice a week. He loves it even though he still won't put his head in the water.

He is sleeping in his own room without Jesse. He can't decide whether to be on the floor or in the bed but that's okay. I have been getting up with him once a night, most nights but it hasn't been too bad. He's learning to play Jesse's new Play Station video game. It's good for fine-motor skills. At least, that's my story and I'm sticking to it! Jesse is happy to have his own room to sleep in.

June 26, 2002

Andrew is kind of out of it today. He and Jesse have fought a lot. I tried to play trains with him but it was so frustrating. I can see why kids may not want to play with him. He told me what to play with and how to do it. Once, he said I couldn't have the caboose. He grabbed it off my train, yelling at me. I guess if I was to look at the positive, I can say that his language skills are improving. His tolerance level hasn't. He gets angry fairly easily but today was something just a little different.

I sense more frustration – he got close to tears many times and did start crying once. I think it's more than just being tired. He has slept well for a full week. He must need something he's not getting. The days are pretty much the same, and they haven't had any other kids to play with for nearly a month. That makes it hard. And most of Andrew's stuff is still packed. Perhaps we haven't done anything new lately. It's something to think about.

June 27, 2002

This has to be a first. Jesse got angry with Andrew tonight because Andrew was "talking too much." He has turned into a chatterbox lately. He tells us who is playing on his computer baseball game or about his trains. Sometimes it is movie talk but sometimes it's not. He is really communicating well.

June 28, 2002

Andrew and Jesse had an introduction session to the Language Camp that starts next Tuesday. The camp director was very positive and feels both boys will do great. Unfortunately, Andrew's tolerance level is still very low. I think both boys will do better when they can meet some neighborhood kids to play with. I sure have been struggling lately. I mostly feel angry with Andrew, although Jesse gets it, too. I can't believe how well Andrew is talking, and yet, I get so irritated! I know I'm not helping.

I think he needs more attention than I want to give him and I feel resentful. I'm not a good model for this new level of development. He looked at me the other day and said angrily, "I could just smack you." Of course, that made me madder. Yet, at another level, I was horrified. I don't have to ask where he heard that. I've said it numerous times out loud either to him or to myself. I would never do it, but he kind of knows what it means. I can't believe he said it!

July 1, 2002

Yesterday we went to both worship service and Sunday School so Andrew was at church for three hours. He did very well. He has been sleeping well. His favorite thing to do is play baseball: nerf ball inside, wiffleball outside, or on the computer. Language Camp begins tomorrow. He started to eat corn on the cob after four months of working on it.

July 2, 2002

Today was the first day of Language Camp. Andrew did very well. He had no trouble separating from me and seemed to do fine with the extra kids and adults. Jesse thinks that his being there helped. He's probably right.

July 4, 2002

I'm so incredibly thankful that God was watching over Andrew tonight. We went to a July 4th cookout at the house of one of Donald's friends. It's out in the country; a big house with a pond some 100 feet in front of the house. While we were getting our food in the backyard, Andrew started walking around the side of the house towards the front yard. Donald went to call him back. As he was calling to Andrew, he saw him disappear. He had reached the edge of the pond and had fallen forward into the water. It must have been shallow because, although Andrew was totally wet, he was able to get himself out. If he hadn't, there was no way Donald would have been able to reach him in time. He would have drowned!

I'm still in a state of shock. It happened so quickly. The pond was at least 100 feet away, on the other side of the house. What was he doing over there, and how did he get there so quickly? How glad I am that Donald went after him. Andrew was soaked and very scared. All I can think to do is take a deep breath and thank God over and over for saving him.

July 5, 2002

Donald and I painted in our new house today. When we got back to Mema's to pick up the boys, Andrew saw paint on my legs. He said, "Daddy, did you paint Mommy?" What good, independent thinking!

July 19, 2002

Andrew did not sleep well last night. He got the trains he took to bed taken away for talking. He finally fell asleep after a few minutes of crying. He kept crying out and arguing in his sleep. I lay down with him at 1 a.m. He was fitful and moving around. He cried out twice but quickly settled down when I reassured him I was there. He fell into a deep sleep and slept through the rest of the night. I stayed with him from 1-3 a.m. He was fine today.

Andrew loves his own room and our new house. He has enjoyed playing baseball in the front yard and riding his tricycle around the coves. He has had some general behavioral issues since we've moved in on the 9th: not obeying, yelling, and temper tantrums. Perhaps he finally got tired of the transitions. He seems to have calmed down some. I haven't been very consistent with his vitamins since we moved in. I need to do better. Most nights he gets one teaspoon of calcium and three-fourth teaspoon of SNT vitamins – all in one dose. I hope it's better than nothing.

July 21, 2002

Andrew really struggled this morning getting ready for church. He wouldn't cooperate. Donald had to force him to get dressed. It was the first time in a long time that Andrew could not be talked into cooperating. Of course, we didn't have a lot of time to be patient and wait it out. He did fine once he got to church and settled into playing. He also went across the monkey bars at the park by himself for the first time. He is very proud of himself and didn't want to get off!

July 25, 2002

I met with the principal at the elementary school. She will talk with the curriculum coordinator for Andrew's placement with the special education teacher and the general education teacher. An IEP won't be available for the first month, but she will personally see to his placement. An SL and an OT won't be available until after the IEP meeting. We will be called as soon as she knows more information.

I will bring Andrew up to the school next Wednesday to meet the principal and to tour the school. Overall, it was a very positive meeting. I'm disappointed that the IEP meeting won't happen before school starts, but I feel everything possible is being done to ensure a smooth transition.

July 30, 2002

Andrew is Andrew. The emotional roller-coaster ride has been pretty intense these past few weeks. On the upside, his ability to communicate continues to steadily improve. We have been amazed at the information he can share and the quality of his speech. He has only had a few big meltdowns. He is sleeping well.

On the flip side, he has become much more rigid in his routine: What he will do and what he will eat. He yells if I try to get him to do or eat anything different. His delay in social skills is painfully obvious when other kids are around. He will acknowledge people and even shake hands if asked. But he just doesn't know how to play *with* other kids, and he gets overwhelmed if we have more than four kids over.

I'm taking him to the school tomorrow to meet the principal and look around the school. Hopefully, I'll learn where he will be placed and how it will work. There's no way to get the IEP done before school starts so we have to try for the next best thing – a great placement. School starts in two weeks. It's our next big hurdle.

August 6, 2002

I'm baffled by Andrew's lack of eating any variety of foods he used to eat. He's not even eating bread with honey! It has been difficult to watch him trying to play with other kids. We have at least twelve kids in our immediate neighborhood between the ages of four and eleven. Most days there are three or four at our house. One day, we had five kids plus Andrew in our playroom. He walked out and went outside. It was too much for him. (The boys are so much noisier and rambunctious than the girls.) The kids have already told me that they can't understand what Andrew says and that he isn't playing with them.

I'm nervous about how well he is going to do in a school classroom with lots of kids. His tolerance for unmet needs is still not great. But we never know what is going to set him off. Twice this week I've taken him to a store only to have him throw a fit because I got the "wrong" cart. He wouldn't walk with me, wouldn't get in the cart, and yelled loud enough to catch a lot of people's attention. I know we need to be doing things like taking him to the store but I confess, it's easier to leave him at home.

We went to the children's museum with his Language Camp group. Andrew cried and yelled. He didn't want to go in. Once in, he kept running away from the clinician. I hadn't planned on staying but had to. I tried to stay out of the way as much as possible. It was a miserable experience for the most part. I think Jesse would have enjoyed it more if he hadn't been embarrassed by Andrew's behavior.

We have been visiting the same church for six weeks and Andrew has done very well in his class. He usually throws a fit about going to church but once there, he does fine. This Sunday was the first time they had to get me. He had a great morning but then something happened. The teacher didn't know what. In the middle of story time, Andrew got up and became loud and disruptive. He wouldn't quiet down. When they tried to do a craft project, he threw things and hit the teacher. So they came and got me.

The sad part is, and I didn't tell them this, I didn't know what to do either. He yelled at me, was mad I was there, and told me to go away. I sat down in a chair that he couldn't see. So when he looked up, he thought I'd left, which made him cry. He cried for ten minutes even as I was holding him.

In some ways he is doing so well. In others, it is obvious we have a long way to go. I can't help but wonder if he will ever be able to compensate for all the things that he struggles with. He seems to make progress in one area while regressing in another. It almost feels like we have to choose what area he will do well in at the expense of other areas. I've heard of a place around here that offers hippotherapy, but I wonder if he has already gained what he can out of that. Perhaps he needs play therapy? I don't know.

He has been throwing himself onto the floor more lately, loves doing somersaults over and over without stopping, and sometimes just runs around in a circle. We've had him on the trampoline a lot and he likes that. He won't get on the two-wheel bicycle because he thinks it isn't his and it's "too high." We may have to get a new bike. Then, there are his socks. He pulls them up so often and so high that he is stretching them all out. We can't get him to leave them alone.

I'm not sure where we are to go from here other than to get him established in school. Maybe that's a big enough adjustment for him without adding anything else at this point. He won't get any SL or OT from the school until we have the IEP. He did well at Language Camp although I can't see any obvious changes or improvements. I'm not sure how much it helped but I know it didn't hurt.

August 9, 2002

UM Language Camp summary report:

Summer Language Camp was an intensive program designed to provide opportunities to develop communication skills in the therapy setting and then apply those skills in community outings. Group center activities incorporated individual language goals into each task and consisted of role-play, art, games, and food preparation. Off-task behaviors (of Andrew's) included excessive talking over others, lying on the floor, leaving the seat, and carrying a blanket or hat. These behaviors were significantly diminished through the use of verbal redirection, a "quiet" visual, offering choices, facilitated seating, and tactile objects (stress ball, hand exerciser, rubber twisty) to manipulate. A tactile object to manipulate and facilitative foods during the story writing task were beneficial to maintain attention and decrease excessive talking.

Community outings seemed to be overwhelming due to increased visual and auditory stimuli. Andrew's reactions included running away, seeking comfort of being held by mother, attempting to hide, and yelling. Due to a previously identified aversion to bodily contact in the form of deep pressure to the shoulders or the buddy hug, strategies used for staying with the group consisted of hand-holding, increased requirements and limit setting in graded steps, positive reinforcement for improvements, verbal redirection and providing verbal choices. Verbal and visual preparation (social stories) in advance aided transitioning to new activities including outings.

Parent involvement included daily reporting about the day's activities, one observation of a session, and participation in all field trips. Progress was noted. Continued language therapy is recommended to focus on reporting on recent events with more detail, answering "why" and "how" questions, and seeking information from a peer. A parent phone conference was held August 9 with Mrs. Simpson. Progress and recommendations were discussed, and Mrs. Simpson indicated agreement. It was recommended that implementation of the above strategies (social stories, manipulatives, choices, facilitative seating, use of visuals, graded steps) be used to support success in an inclusive school environment.

Starting Kindergarten: We've Been Working Towards This Day

❖

(August 2002 – November 2002)

August 12, 2002

Today is the first day of school. Andrew had a tough morning but did okay once we got to school. I'm not too concerned about how he will do this week. The kindergarten class is divided up so that each child only goes one day this week, so there are only four kids each day to learn the routine and teacher, Ms. Ebbers. They are allowing Andrew to go every day. Next Monday when all sixteen kids are there will be the most interesting and scary. I'm afraid he'll be overwhelmed.

I can't believe he is in kindergarten. We've spent the past three years getting him ready for this day. I think we have all done a pretty good job, considering where we started.

August 13, 2002

Ms. Ebbers called. She said the speech therapist came to the class and tried to talk with Andrew. He was on the computer and didn't cooperate. The school's behavioral specialist also came by to observe him. Ms. Ebbers "pushed" Andrew a little more today and was told to "go away." Andrew loves the *Arthur* computer game and shuts the world out when he plays it. At lunch, he finishes eating and then runs around the cafeteria. He won't stay in his seat. I need to put his snack in the side pocket of his backpack and not in his lunchbox.

I received a phone call from the curriculum coordinator at the school. Several people observed Andrew in the classroom today. She said he was "so bright but overwhelmed." She is concerned about his being overstimulated when all the kids get there next week. She wants to keep him in the general education class as much as possible but may need to pull him out at times to help him stay focused. The autism team has been called to do some observation. They will do that either Wednesday or Thursday.

August 16, 2002

Note from school:

Andrew came in and did the morning work after one request. We have been doing two art activities that require me painting their hands. He let me paint his hands today! When I asked, he said, "okay," but when I started to paint, he wasn't sure about it. But he did do both things – the puzzle is in the folder. The other is a surprise. We are working on a picture cue schedule. Two areas where I need advice are: (a) does he take a nap at home? and (b) how do we help him be quiet in the hallway? We are going to have a sticker or some incentive chart next week. I think that will help.

I did get a chance to read his file today. I'll start the spiral notebook next week. Please call me any time you need to touch base. It has been a good week. Andrew is a sweetie. It is going to be a great year!

August 18, 2002

I gave Andrew a banana. It's the first one in over four months. He was very excited. We'll watch him for the next few days for any reactions.

We went to a church today that we are interested in enough to go back next week. Donald didn't get to go to the service because of Andrew. As soon as we turned into the church's parking lot, he said, "This isn't the right one!" He went into a tantrum from there. Unfortunately, we only made the decision to go this morning so there wasn't any time to prepare him. He cried and cried but eventually settled down, but he never got to where Donald could leave him.

At school, they had a member of the county autism team come out and observe Andrew last week. They are sending an assistant for him tomorrow when all sixteen kids will be there. I am so relieved. Every day last week, he did a little better, but when all the kids get there at once, it will be like starting over. His teacher is wonderful but she can't handle fifteen kids plus Andrew on her own. We don't know how long the assistant will last, but it's a step in the right direction. We have been very pleased with the effort the school has made for both the boys. It is a wonderful feeling to know we've made a good choice in schools on their behalf.

August 19, 2002

Today was the first day that all the kindergartners were in school. Andrew had a rough morning. The head of the autism team, Dr. A., spent most of the morning working with Andrew in the classroom. He didn't want to get off the computer (imagine that). When she (Dr. A.) gave Andrew the choice of doing his book or her holding him, he ran over to the bookcase and started climbing it. So, of course, she had to hold him. That caused his behavior to escalate even more. He ran over to the window and lightly banged his head against it. He finally regrouped and ended up doing his bookwork.

There are four computers in the classroom. He has a favorite that he has claimed as his. He doesn't want anyone else using it. When the other kids are using the computer, he walks back and forth behind them, talking. He wants them to all be on the same "page" doing the same thing and gets worked up when they're not. If it weren't so sad, it would be funny.

Dr. A. and the school have assigned a behavioral specialist assistant to work with Andrew every morning from 8 a.m. to noon for up to four weeks. They are setting up a picture sequence to help him with the order in which to do things and to help make choices. They are going to put a beanbag in a remote corner of the room for him to go to when he needs time to regroup. The hope is that will get him the proprioceptive input he needs at the time so he doesn't have to bang his head or climb things.

They commented that it is obvious that Andrew is smart. They really want to work with him so that he can stay in the general education class. However, going to the special education class for the bookwork is still a possibility if these other things don't help him make the adjustments. The afternoons are going better; he does well at lunch, rest time, and centers (choosing to play in the kitchen area, with blocks, or on the computer). It is mainly during the academic portion of the day that he struggles. I continue to be very pleased with the effort the school is making to help Andrew and also to keep in communication with us about what's going on.

August 20, 2002

Note from school:

We had fire, tornado, earthquake, and intruder drills today. Andrew did well. The behavioral specialist came and worked with Andrew to keep him on task. There was good participation in gym. We're going to implement the 1-2-3 Magic program to encourage compliance in classroom activities.

[Author's note: *1-2-3 Magic* is a discipline program by Dr. Thomas Phelan that is used by parents, teachers, and caregivers. For more information, visit www.parent-magic.com]

August 21, 2002

Note from school:

Andrew appeared to have more difficulty complying with directives this morning. I am using lots of praise, redirection, prompting, and 1-2-3 Magic during the course of the day. I am putting together a visual schedule that we hope will be helpful to Andrew in making transitions in the classroom. Thanks for the quiet sign.

August 26, 2002

We have been so pleased with the school here. They are implementing several strategies. They are working on a visual schedule so Andrew can visually anticipate the next thing to do. It also helps him understand when he will get to do his favorite things – like snack and computer time. They have brought in a big beanbag chair that sits in a corner of the room. When he feels overwhelmed, he is allowed to go there to regroup. Sinking into the chair gives him that deep pressure around his back and shoulders (proprioceptive) he needs to calm down.

He finally had the meltdown we've been anticipating. (We call what he does a "meltdown." It seems to describe it best.) It's been a tough weekend, and this morning it hit. (I had warned his teacher that it was coming.) He refused to go to school. (Yesterday was a nightmare at church, too, but that's another story.) He knows that they are going to push him, try to get him to do things he doesn't want to do, things that are hard for him. He comes home tired and yet, like most kids, with a new energy for doing what he wants to do ... finally!

I confess that it is very difficult for Donald and me right now. We know that this is the best thing for him. He has so much potential.

They have to push him some or he'll never realize that potential. Yet, his yelling and running away (that dissolves into heartbreaking sobs and hiding his face) breaks our own hearts. We aren't so much angry at his temper tantrums as we are hurt for the fear behind the tantrums.

I am so thankful for all the prayers that are said on Andrew's and our behalf. I *know* they have made a huge difference in how Andrew has handled all the transitions that come with a major move. He really has done incredibly well, so much better than we were anticipating. And this bump in the road lately is just that – a bump in the road. He is communicating much better, expressing independent thought, getting along better with his brother, wanting to "help" around the house, and trying to play with the neighborhood kids. It is amazing how much he has accomplished in the past six months.

Being near extended family has been good for Donald and me, too. We've been very fortunate not to have the marital problems that often seem to come with having a special needs kid. It is nice to be able to have time for each other and not worry about who is watching Andrew.

August 27, 2002

Note from school:

Andrew did a good job during circle. He transitioned well with prompting in the morning. He had one outburst with inappropriate vocalization this morning. It was much shorter in duration. Andrew's visual schedule is completed. We also began using a "quiet game" in an effort to decrease his inappropriate verbal outbursts. I observed Andrew smiling throughout the day. Andrew is learning that a "touch" on his shoulder is a "reminder" to not talk out loud. He is responding well to this method and is tolerating light, firm touch.

August 30, 2002

Andrew's IEP meeting is this afternoon. They have already informed us of what they will be proposing. They want Andrew to start out in the general education class for the first thirty minutes each day. Then, for academics in the morning, he will go for a few hours to the special education classroom. At lunch, he will rejoin the regular class for the rest of the day.

He has done okay in the general education classroom but he is not handling the instructional part well. That's when he is supposed to sit at his desk quietly, work on his workbooks with time limits and verbal instructions. He just can't do that. They have brought in a behavioral specialist to help him each morning. It has helped, but it won't be enough. We hope this will allow Andrew to keep up with the academics without the pressure and disruptions of the regular classroom. Donald and I are pleased with the efforts the school has made and continues to make on behalf of the boys. They really want it to work. It gives us hope that this will work for them both. We'll see.

IEP meeting notes:

First the team members were introduced. The team then reviewed Andrew's progress since coming to the school and also went over his previous program. Goals and objectives were developed in the area of readiness, prevocational skills, and speech. The team wants Andrew in the regular program for whatever amount of time is appropriate for him. He is currently having difficulty with the academic instruction in the classroom. The team recommends Expanded Resource so that Andrew can receive special instruction on his level of functioning. The resource teacher, Mrs. Brewer, shared specific information about Andrew's program and procedures used the classroom.

The team recommends that Andrew participate in music, P.E., lunch, recess, unit time, centers, nap, and dismissal as well as early-bird and calendar in the regular kindergarten class. Language goals were developed that will be incorporated into his total program. The team recommends working on fine-motor skills during art time because the art expectations are not appropriate for him. The team recommends direct services for academics in Expanded Resource, speech pullout, and OT consultation.

[Author's note: There is a debate concerning whether children with special needs should be fully included in a general classroom setting or if they should be placed strictly in a special education classroom. It is my opinion that each family must work with the school system to decide what is best for their child and family based on their goals and needs. I do not believe that this is a "one-size-fits-all" decision.]

September 3, 2002

Note from school:

What a good day! Andrew has made some new friends in Mrs. Brewer's class. He had very few problems with transitioning to the new classroom and really likes his "new teachers." He had a great time playing and learning with peers.

September 6, 2002

Note from school:

Andrew found his way from Ms. Ebbers' to Mrs. Brewer's classroom all by himself! We drew a map just in case. He was very proud of himself, and we were proud of him also.

September 9, 2002

Note from school, Mrs. Brewer:

I am very happy with Andrew's transition to my class. He seems to be very happy. He is cooperative during his lessons and does his work well. We really enjoy him. Andrew had a hard time settling down this afternoon. He was very silly, throwing things, and trying to be "chased."

September 20, 2002

Yesterday I was very frustrated with the boys. It was raining, and they were so rambunctious. We had turned off the Play Station and computer because of the storms. I felt at my wit's end. They play for a short while. Then someone gets mad, and the yelling and hitting starts. I'm amazed that my mom put up with me and my three siblings. I only have two kids to deal with and find it hard at times.

September 22, 2002

We are still working on the play structure for the backyard. We have the ladders built and the slide attached. Andrew was so excited, you'd think it was already Christmas. (We told him it was an early Christmas present.) We could have stopped right then; the boys were thrilled. But of course, there's more. It has been fun working on it as a family. Even the dogs get into it by wrestling each other right where we are trying to work. It will be great to have it done.

September 26, 2002

Note from school:

Andrew was "wired" when he came back this afternoon. He had his hands and feet on his friends – getting in their faces. He pushed one girl into the wall and said she started it. Then he hit her with his lunchbox (in her face). He is excited about his birthday and I'm not sure if his excitement "carried over." We had our AR (accelerated reader) treat today. Andrew had popcorn and a sugar cookie.

September 27, 2002

My sweet Andrew is six years old today. He is such a joy. This is the first year he has been able to anticipate his birthday and count the days. He is so excited. We are trying to make it a very special day. He is doing so well. Yes, he is behind the other kids, but how far he has come! He talks with us, laughs, and plays. He sometimes asks questions and still loves to cuddle. There are rough times but rarely tough days. That is a tremendous blessing and to think he will continue to improve! Perhaps it means so much because he has had to fight so hard for it.

September 29, 2002

It's been a trying weekend. I haven't felt well, Jesse has had an attitude problem and Andrew has been testy. Both boys are fine if we cooperate with their wishes. As soon as there is a hint of us saying "wait," "no," or "please do," the problems begin. They have both been argumentative, whiny, and disrespectful. It's hard to be firm but understanding, and it's mentally and emotionally tiring.

October 2, 2002

I am sitting here in tears; happy, happy tears. My Andrew, my sweet boy, just came up and gave me a hug and said, "I love you." This is the first time he has spoken those words on his own, with no prompting. It was totally out of the blue. Oh, what a happy, happy day this is! I'm undone by three little words.

October 7, 2002

Andrew is doing fairly well. I think we're hitting another rough patch with him, though. He has been yelling a lot and trying to manipulate. I guess this is the next step. Our challenge is coming up with an appropriate, immediate consequence. For example, he throws a fit as we are trying to leave for school. I can't give him a consequence after school because he doesn't make the connection between his morning behavior and afternoon consequence. But if we give him a time-out, we might make Jesse late for school. It's a challenge.

He is communicating with us fairly well. He still quotes movies and can only answer questions if you phrase them the correct way. His diet has become even more limited than it was before. (He is rejecting some of his old favorites and hasn't replaced them with new ones.) But he almost always sleeps through the night. He has only been sick once since we've moved. He is responding well to timers and rewards. We've seen steady progress, although I can't always put into words what the progress is. It just is. He's also growing like crazy and is getting so tall. He makes great eye contact, greets people, and gives the best hugs.

We are so thrilled to be here in Tennessee. This move has been very good for all of us. The support Donald's family has given us already is amazing. I've never lived near extended family and can only now appreciate the benefits. We have been very, very blessed.

[Author's note: One of the best courses of action a family can take following the diagnosis of a disorder/disability is to surround itself with supportive people. Ideally, this support will come from other family members. However, support can also come from friends, teachers, doctors, therapists, and support groups.]

October 17, 2002

About an hour after dinner (cheese pizza and chips) last night, Andrew started complaining of his stomach hurting and itching. He had a bout of diarrhea. When we got his clothes off, he had a rash: Little bumps appeared and red splotchy patches – mostly on his back but a few on his belly, head, neck, and upper legs. Then his ears turned red. He didn't have any other symptoms. Aunt Paula came over to look at the rash. She hadn't seen anything quite like it, she said. We used calamine lotion to help the itching. His stomach stopped hurting as soon as he finished in the bathroom. This morning, the rash and bumps were gone. He felt fine. We think perhaps it was some kind of hives. (Cousin Holly got hives for no apparent reason when she was younger). We'll see how he does the rest of the day. It was pretty strange.

October 18, 2002

I saw one of the assistants in Andrew's resource class. She said Andrew had a fantastic week and is doing well. He is reading great, and he did all his work so there is no carry-over to the next week. We love those good reports.

October 19, 2002

I'm emotionally tired and cried out, I think. Yet, at the same time, if I was given the chance, I could tear a room apart. I guess the anger isn't gone yet. I haven't cried this hard in a long time. Andrew. Sometimes, it just hurts so much.

I took him to the birthday party of one of the girls in his kindergarten class. It was a nightmare. He was already being oppositional when we left the house. But he was also excited to go to the party and he had calmed down by the time we got there. It was held at a gymnasium where cheerleaders practice. There were probably twenty or more kids – all five- and six-years-old. They spent the first hour jumping and tumbling and climbing. Andrew wouldn't do it. I guess he got overwhelmed by the number of kids and the large, new environment. He sat by me and any time someone tried to talk to him, including me, he just yelled "no!" at us. He would scoot close to me but I wasn't allowed to hold him or even put my arm around him.

When the kids went to another room, Andrew and I were left alone. That's when he got up and started tumbling and doing some of the things the kids had been doing. He got mad when I wouldn't let him jump or climb but I knew we weren't supposed to be in there by ourselves. I needed him to stay close. Later he did okay with sitting and having cake and ice cream, but then it was time to open presents.

The birthday girl was opening them fairly quickly with all the kids crowded around. Andrew wanted to pick a present. The girl's mother thought Andrew wanted to choose which one she would open next, so she let Andrew pick one. Well, Andrew wanted to pick one that he could open. When I tried to explain that he couldn't open one because it wasn't his birthday, he got mad. He decided it was time to go home and started to leave. When I told him to stop, he started yelling again. I got our stuff and we slipped out the back while presents were still being opened.

I held it together at the party but as soon as we got in the van, I started bawling. It just all came out. I know we need to take Andrew places and let him do things like parties, but I hate them and I dread them. They remind me of how different he is. I don't want to be reminded. People say don't compare kids and while it's true I shouldn't, it's impossible not to. People are always comparing their kids. You hope it doesn't have a negative effect and that you don't push your own child to be perfect. But on days like today when I see so many other kids Andrew's age – it breaks my heart. He is different. He is "behind." I think he may always be and I hate it.

So, I guess I still haven't accepted it. I'm still angry about it. I rejoice in his improvements and progress. Truly, I do. It's just that every now and then, it hits. And it is hard. I don't want people to talk me out of it or make light of it or make me feel guilty for my feelings. I'm thankful that Donald let me cry on his shoulder and talk through it, like he always does. There's nothing else to do but try to get some good rest tonight and go at it again in the morning – and to keep taking deep breaths.

November 25, 2002

Andrew has both ears infected. His doctor commented that he must have a high threshold of pain. The one ear Andrew said hurt is bulging. The ear that he said didn't hurt was very red and infected. The ear infections tell us why he was so belligerent this weekend. Wow. He hasn't had ear infections in so long, I'd almost forgotten about them – almost.

Stuck:
Is This as Good as It Gets?

❖

(December 2002 – February 2003)

December 8, 2002

Andrew has struggled the past few weeks with yelling, being argumentative, disobeying, etc. We are going to get very strict with his diet
again to see if it helps. It is either his diet that is causing this behavior
or else it's the regression that usually occurs before he makes a breakthrough in some area. Why do the breakthroughs have to come at such
a high price?

December 11, 2002

I talked with Mrs. Brewer. Andrew fell asleep in Ms. Ebbers' class and
woke up crying and disoriented. He sat on her lap and cried for several
minutes and then settled down. She said he was upset earlier today as well.

December 21, 2002

Andrew has been congested. He is beginning to cough and run a temperature of 101 degrees. He is having a hard time getting well again.

December 24, 2002

I took Andrew to the doctor for fever, cough, congestion, and an ear
hurting. It was a nightmare. He wouldn't leave the patient's room to be
weighed. He screamed, kicked, and tried to run out of the clinic. I finally settled him down a little but when the doctor came in, he screamed
again. "Stop touching me!" It's a wonder she was able to check him out
at all. He does have an ear infected.

It took everything I had not to cry in front of everyone. It was extremely embarrassing and I felt so helpless. I couldn't make him understand that we were only trying to help him.

Christmas 2002

Andrew is six years, three months old. My, how time flies. He still seems to be stuck in between cooperation and angry rebellion. His favorite Christmas gift this year was a large Buzz Lightyear. He also loves the LeapFrog Learning System, Play Station and computer games. He is living off jelly sandwiches (when did he stop eating peanut butter?), chips, popsicles, and lemonade.

December 30, 2002

It is a blessing to see Jesse and Andrew playing well together. I remember only two years ago when it seemed like they would never get along. It's getting better and I'm glad.

January 3, 2003

Andrew's ears don't hurt, but he has had a headache the past two days. Yesterday was pretty severe. After he woke up from a nap, he cried and cried. It took a while for the medicine to help. In the meantime, he wanted the lights out and as little noise as possible. Maybe he had a migraine? He is better today.

January 5, 2003

Andrew missed two Sundays at church, so this morning was not fun. He refused to go into his classroom. He insisted "they don't like me." He still mixes up his pronouns so he meant to say, "I don't like them." It took twenty minutes and a sucker to get him to calm down so I could leave. He made the transition to second hour fine. Then, during the sermon, we could hear him. "Don't touch me! I said leave me alone!" Donald had to go settle him down.

Andrew has been "stuck" since Thanksgiving. We are both tired and frustrated at his lack of progress lately – behaviorally. Once again we are asking ourselves, "Is this as good as it gets?" I don't think so, but at times Donald and I are both losing hope that he will be able to cope 100% some day. Andrew is making progress but it is so slow that he is losing ground on his peers every day. My heart feels heavy. How long will we struggle with him? At what point do we draw the line between making him (and others) miserable and just giving in?

January 7, 2003

It was a rough morning with Andrew. He didn't want to get dressed or go to school. I become tired of his yelling and running from me. I can't physically make him do anything, so it's almost impossible to get him to cooperate when he doesn't want to. It makes me so angry. I feel as stuck as Andrew has been. I'm angry that Donald can plan for a job change but I can't. I don't have a choice. I can't walk away from parenting my special needs child.

On that note, I put my pen down and called Mom. We talked for almost an hour with Dad listening in. It was very helpful. I'm so thankful for the support. The circumstances haven't changed, but I feel better just letting off some steam. I don't think I'm so much angry at Donald as I am frustrated with feeling stuck. I've never liked that feeling or thinking that I don't have choices.

January 8, 2003

Note from school:

Andrew was "argumentative" today. There were lots of no's. He played rough on the playground, "throwing" kids down.

January 19, 2003

The service ran overtime at church this morning. We could hear Andrew from the sanctuary, and he sounded distressed. When I went to get him, he was standing there crying. I didn't recognize any of the adults. (The regular teacher had taken a child to the restroom.) There were a few older kids in the room waiting for their parents and causing a lot of commotion. Andrew got overwhelmed. Something has got to change.

January 22, 2003

I'm sitting in the airport waiting for Mom's flight. It's good to get away for a little while. I've really been struggling with Andrew's behavior lately. I feel frustrated because it seems that he should be doing better than he is. It's so hard to stay patient when confronted by his temper tantrums and his lack of attention and understanding. But I know that is exactly what I need to be – patient – if he is to grow and learn how to cope. I just wish I had a better understanding of how much he understands. What should my expectations be? I don't want them to be too low so he doesn't reach his potential. Neither do I want them to be too high so that we both end up frustrated by his inability to reach them.

January 30, 2003
Note from school:

Andrew "walked" off from the playground three times, and I verbally persuaded him to come back twice. The third time I had to carry him back. When we got in, he walked out of our room and refused to come back. We called Mrs. Brewer to help. The morning was fine.

January 31, 2003
I had a meeting with Mrs. Sheri, the children's minister at our church. Andrew is having difficulty transitioning from first service to second. We've come up with the idea of getting a yellow beanbag chair for the classroom. Mrs. Sheri is also going to try to get a Thomas train for Andrew to play with. Finally, we will only bring Andrew to the first service until his stress level lowers overall (church, school, home).

Note from school:

As of today, we are going to provide extra assistance for Andrew during recess and centers in the classroom. An assistant from my class (Mrs. Brewer's) will be with him to provide guidance and encouragement for appropriate play and social activities during these times. This will hopefully help with maintaining his safety and securing that he is always appropriately monitored. Please contact me if you have any questions.

P.S. We can discuss this and other concerns in more depth at our upcoming multi-personnel team meeting.

February 2, 2003
We walked into the Sunday School room, and there was the yellow beanbag chair and a Thomas train you can pull. Andrew was thrilled. I was amazed. We had only met Friday at lunch. How did Mrs. Sheri get those things so quickly? It's support like that which helps us feel like we can deal with all this.

February 7, 2003

The kids were home Monday through Wednesday with a fever. Then school was cancelled yesterday because of snow. Finally, today is a day to get things done away from the house. God was gracious this week and has given me an extra amount of patience and endurance, especially when Andrew and I were awake Thursday morning from 3:00-5:30.

This morning, Andrew couldn't get himself together enough to get to school on time. I had to take him a few minutes late, which necessitated a visit to the front office first. It did not go well. Any time we have to bend the rules a little to compensate for Andrew's needs, there is always someone who gets bent out of shape. I had already had a bad morning trying to get Andrew to where he would cooperate. I didn't need that.

I waited twenty minutes in the office (after getting Andrew settled in his class) to speak with the principal. She was wonderful. I had barely explained the situation when she was assuring me that she would take care of everything, and she did. I so appreciate how she handled everything. It made me feel that I'd been heard, that I was being taken seriously, and that Andrew is important. It makes all the difference to have that kind of support.

February 10, 2003

IEP meeting notes:

A pamphlet explaining parent rights was offered. The purpose of the meeting was stated. The OT reported on her recent observation and report. This contained several suggestions. The autism team has provided several examples of Social Stories. Mrs. Brewer, Expanded Resource, reported on the behavior plan currently in place. The behavior consultant presented a behavioral support plan. This plan was discussed at length. Several amendments were made. No change to the IEP was made. We will get information on summer programs.

February 11, 2003

My discontentment has surfaced again. The whole staying-home issue, motherhood issue. Andrew is sick again. Last week, both boys were sick for three days. Then on Sunday evening, Andrew got really sick – 102 degree fever and vomiting. I catnapped from 11:30 p.m. to 5:00 a.m. Jesse also stayed home Monday. It turns out Andrew has strep throat with one red ear. He was put on Amoxicillin and has to stay home tomorrow. I'm fighting an upper-respiratory infection, which adds to my being very tired.

I know I don't deal with things well when I'm tired. This time was no exception. I don't know why God has allowed Andrew to be autistic. I don't know why He wants me to be Jesse and Andrew's mother. Surely there are other women out there who would be a better mother than I am. Yet, here I am, and it's a life sentence since I will always be their mother. Does that have to be a bad thing? No, of course not. I just need to let go of whatever other plans I might have had for my life.

February 12, 2003

The fever is gone. Andrew is mad that we won't let him go to school. He is "star of the week." We can't let him go because he is still contagious from the strep throat but just try to get him to understand!

February 13, 2003

Andrew is complaining of leg pain and that he "can't walk." It started in the middle of the night. I'm not sure what's going on. He loved showing his poster of pictures to his classmates as the star of the week. He also took his big Buzz Lightyear as his favorite toy. Tonight, he tried to fall asleep at 6:10 p.m. His stomach was hurting. He started itching around 7:30 p.m. with a slight rash. I gave him Benadryl, which was a real fight. (It didn't look or taste "right" to him.) He finally fell asleep.

February 16, 2003

It was a struggle to get Andrew to Sunday School again. Apparently, Aunt Paula heard him during the first service. They got Donald (he's helping with the third-grade class), and he took Andrew and Jesse home. I wish it wasn't such a struggle to have Andrew there. I wish I knew what to do to help him. Maybe I need to stay with him during the whole hour. We've got to keep bringing him to church. I just don't know what our expectations should be. I'm trying not to worry about it. I'm trying not to worry about anything except taking things one day at a time.

February 17, 2003

The kids are home today because of President's Day. We're doing okay, but it seems like an ever-present struggle. Andrew woke up in one of his moods. It was a survival day. We're already looking into plans for this summer. He won't be eligible for the school's summer program, and we won't be doing the Language Camp again. We might look into the hippotherapy for a while. Plus, we signed up the boys for baseball (Jesse) and t-ball (Andrew), which begins in May. Donald is going to help with Andrew's team. It should be interesting and fun.

February 18, 2003

It's been another rough night with Andrew. It was time to take a bath and he refused. He hit, yelled, and ran from us. We tried to give him the choice between bath and going straight to bed but that didn't work. So we put him to bed. *Then* he was ready to comply. We didn't let him have his bath. He is still on his bed.

I hope we did the right thing. I hope he can truly understand the consequences and what he did to cause them. If not, it was a hard night for nothing. But what else can we do? He knew what we wanted and he refused to obey. There had to be a consequence. We can't just let him keep hitting us.

It's hard. I don't want to let Andrew get away with abusive behavior. I'm not always sure when he is being rebellious and when the autism has taken over. Sometimes, I guess wrong. I push him when I should back off. At other times, I back off and excuse him when I should have pushed. I thought it would get easier to work with him as he got older, but so far it hasn't. It has just gotten different.

The ASD Dance:
Two Steps Forward,
One Step Back

❖

(March 2003 – October 2003)

March 13, 2003
We're in Sun City West, Arizona, for spring break. Mom made some notes to summarize where Andrew is these days. His favorite things to eat are applesauce, popsicles, and Goldfish. He loves to blow kisses and blow on the tummies of family members. There is better eye contact and increased social interaction. He still uses "movie talk" but it can be reduced or limited. His favorite movies are *Lion King* and *Peter Pan*. He is 48 pounds and is 48" tall. He's almost a square! We've had a wonderful vacation.

March 17, 2003
Note from school:
Andrew came in today in a wonderful mood and did a spectacular job on his work. He chatted with us with nice conversations. He was very, very pleasant.

March 25, 2003
Note to school:
Ms. Ebbers, I was working with Andrew on his star of the week homework yesterday. He told me that "I like 'Chris' because she is not nice." Since that didn't make sense, I questioned him. He said she isn't nice to him. I tried to get him to think of something he liked about her but he was stuck. He took his pencil and wrote "she is not ni," then looked up at me and asked what the

127

other letters were. I didn't know he could spell that much of the sentence! While I'm thrilled he did so much on his own, I'm not sending the homework in.

April 9, 2003

We had a good time for Jesse's birthday. Andrew was so excited that you'd have thought it was his birthday. He could hardly contain himself as he didn't think Jesse was opening the packages quickly enough. Andrew tried to "help" several times. But really, he did quite well. Jesse was sweet and let Andrew help him.

Andrew is very anxious to play t-ball. His first practice was rained out.

April 15, 2003

I took Andrew to the dentist. I was so proud of him! He let them clean his teeth, floss, and even use the water spray and suction tools. It was great.

April 20, 2003

It's Easter. At least, that's what the calendar says. I have to remember that Easter is what happens in my heart, even if the day doesn't go as planned. We went to Sunday School but had to leave before worship because of Andrew. I was devastated. I really wanted to be in the service, especially since I missed last week when I was sick. He was feeling ornery, his forehead was warm, and he was kicking at the other kids. It was so frustrating. I cried for the limitations put on our family.

April 27, 2003

Andrew has been oppositional this week. It's hard. Yesterday, I'd given Jesse permission to ride his bike up to the school with a friend. Andrew decided to go after them. He rode his bike to the place we said was "far enough." He knew he couldn't go farther on his bike. So he left his bike and started running. A neighbor had to get me since Donald and I were both in the house. I caught Andrew half way to the school.

It's scary that he'll just take off like that. He got mad because I was upset. He has left the house and gone to other people's homes without telling me before. I feel more stressed lately about him and his safety.

We are considering home schooling Jesse next year. I home schooled him for second grade, but we thought we would try the public school when we moved here. He has continually asked me to let him stay home. I confess, I enjoy having both boys at school during the day. I don't know how Andrew would react if he were at school and Jesse stayed home. Andrew is very proud of the fact that they attend the same school. It is something to seriously consider.

April 29, 2003

Note from school:

Andrew's last day will be May 28. The celebrations are done early. Andrew did not have a good day today (morning time). He had a hard time staying on task. He was argumentative and "physical" – running, hitting, and spitting. At lunchtime, he refused to be quiet in the hall, hitting me with his lunchbox and kicking chairs.

May 1, 2003

I had a great talk tonight with Andrew's resource teacher, Mrs. Brewer. She has just gotten back from a conference on autism in Chicago. She said it was wonderful and that she has a lot of questions for me as we look towards next year.

We are 95% sure of Andrew's teacher for next year. Mrs. Bland has a similar personality and teaching style as his current teacher. Andrew has started going to her class three times a week for their circle time. He seems to do well with this. Of course, his assistant is with him.

Mrs. Bland actually requested for Andrew to be in her class. When the first-grade teachers were told to start watching Andrew because "he's coming your way next year," Mrs. Bland was the first to approach Andrew to introduce herself. It didn't go too well. Andrew told her to "be quiet and go away." She was offended at first, but weeks later she told Mrs. Brewer that she would like Andrew in her class. She feels up to the challenge.

Mrs. Brewer has twin boys that are in Andrew's regular class. As it turns out, one of them, Tyler, is Andrew's best buddy. Tyler thinks the world of Andrew. It has already been decided that Tyler will be assigned to Mrs. Bland's class next year, too. They want to keep that friendship intact.

Andrew learns things very quickly, and many times they aren't sure how he has learned them. It may be through large group, small group, or the one-on-one. Mrs. Brewer said he is very smart, but has difficulty applying what he knows.

I'm meeting with Mrs. Brewer next Tuesday so we can get a game plan for next year. Then, we will both request an IEP meeting before the end of the year so that it is set before school starts in August. We continue to be amazed at the length to which the school will go to support Andrew and try to meet his needs. His assistant (Ms. Robin) was able to shadow him on Monday for the kindergarten "field day." It enabled him to participate in several relay races and sit with his class for most of the morning. When he had "had enough," she took him inside to regroup. He was able to join the class again after a little while. Tomorrow is the school parade and award ceremony for the field day events. It will be fun.

Andrew has a few of the preschool Thomas engines (they are smaller than the regular trains). Now he wants a small track that he has seen at Target. We have told him he will have to save his money. So he has been hitting people up for "dollars." He is constantly telling people (family and teachers) that they need to give him a dollar. He is trying to get to $20. Aunt Paula had him help walk their dog and was going to pay him a dollar. She didn't have a dollar bill so she gave him four quarters. He threw a fit! He wants paper dollars, not coins. Most of the time, it's funny. Sometimes, it's annoying. I think he's at $14 right now.

May 8, 2003

Andrew had finally saved up enough "monies" to get the train track he has wanted. So, I took him to Target this afternoon. He proudly gave his stack of one-dollar bills to the cashier. As she handed him his change, he said, "I'm Andrew. Who are you?" It was funny. He is happy with his purchase but is already "in need" of more trains. It's a never-ending need.

May 9, 2003

Andrew was so tired yesterday, he fell asleep by 6:50 p.m. He slept eleven and a half hours! He seems to be okay today.

May 11, 2003

Today we took Andrew's training wheels off his bike. He's a little wobbly, doesn't really know how to stop and has a hard time getting himself started. But hey! He does well when he gets going. It may seem like a little thing to most people but for Andrew, this is a great milestone.

May 14, 2003

Note from school:

Andrew had a time-out today. He and Tyler chased each other. Andrew ran from me three times in the cafeteria (refusing to line up).

May 20, 2003

I am so pleased that Andrew has been in a good place for several days. I often write when I'm frustrated. It's good to know there are good times, too. Like yesterday after school, Andrew had a dish of ice cream and a box of crackers for snack. Then he said, "I'm so hungry. Can I have a popsicle?" I told him, "No. That's enough to eat until dinner. Why don't you get some lemonade?" He said, "I'm not thirsty. I'm popsiclely!"

He snuggled with me last night as we read a book, *Toy Story 2*. He didn't want to read the words himself, but we did talk about what was going on in the pictures. He did so well!

Donald and I are both convinced he needs to be back at the elementary school next year. It is the best thing for him. We have decided to keep Jesse at home after first deciding against it. I realized that I had based the decision on the wrong thing. I didn't say or even think the words, but the message was, "Jesse, I know that home schooling is what you need, but it would be too difficult on Andrew. Therefore, we aren't going to do it."

When did Andrew's needs become more important than Jesse's? They aren't and they never were. We went back and looked at Jesse's needs and decided what was best for him. To us, that means home schooling again. For Andrew, it means public school next year. It might be difficult for him at first. God will just have to give us the wisdom and patience to work it all out.

May 21, 2003

They had Andrew's kindergarten graduation ceremony this morning. He sang the songs and got his diploma. We feel so sentimental when we realize how far he has come. I remember when he first started the preschool program. The goal was to get him ready for kindergarten. Well, he made it. We must be doing something right. Look out, first grade. Here he comes!

May 29, 2003

Yesterday was the last day of school; I guess that means summer is here. I hope it's a good one. I'm trying to make it that way. I want to be able to relax and enjoy the kids. I sat on the bench while Andrew rode his bike. It was a good day.

The decision to home school Jesse next year and beyond is final. I'm actually excited about it now. I think it's just a matter of a year or two before we bring Andrew home as well. He needs so much individual attention. Plus he gets overwhelmed in the classroom; there is always so much going on. If I can home school Jesse, I guess I could home school Andrew, too. Nevertheless, it's a scary thought.

July 3, 2003

Andrew is doing very well. His communication has improved, and he expresses a certain amount of independent thought. He still has two volumes: loud and louder. We are working hard to get him to stop yelling at us but it is slow going. If he yells inappropriately, we fix him with a stare and tell him, "Andrew, you don't have to yell at me." We have found it does not help to yell back.

He really wants to play with everyone and has become quite the tag-along. If he gets overwhelmed, he goes off by himself for some space. It's hard, but we try not to take anything personally.

July 10, 2003

It has been a lazy summer, which is just what we needed. Andrew is doing so well. He has become a tag-along to Jesse, the way little brothers are supposed to. He wants to be in on what the kids in the neighborhood are doing. So far, they seem to accept him. That's wonderful, and most of the time, Jesse isn't too irritated or embarrassed by him. Andrew has gotten very good on his bike, although he did crash the other day and scraped himself badly. He is so affectionate and talks all the time.

I need to be less negative with Andrew. I need to focus less on the autism and delays and more on the positives. He is a sweet, affectionate boy. He tries to communicate as best he can. His gross-motor skills are excellent for an autistic child: riding his bike, kicking a ball, and hitting a baseball. We still have issues with the fine-motor skills: Buttons and zippers are still beyond him. He'll get it eventually; all in good time.

August 11, 2003

Today is the first day of first grade. Andrew received an "E" for conduct, which stands for excellent. It's a great beginning.

August 15, 2003

Note from school:

Andrew is having trouble minding when it is time to clean up and leave the room. He keeps coloring and will not stop.

He has a new fixation this year. He is spinning objects as a form of visual self-stimulation. (That's my opinion.) For example, he holds a pencil between his finger and thumb by the eraser and "spins" it as if stirring a drink. He watches it spin. We have noticed this during the transition between lessons while he is sitting at the table. He is not disturbing others and he stops if you tell him to. I have been offering more appropriate "wait" activities to engage him as a means of redirection. For example, I'll give him a book to look at or a blank paper to draw on. He has done well with the redirection. I would like to see him begin to redirect himself.

August 17, 2003

I've been watching Andrew. Jesse tells me that when Andrew is spinning one object around another, he is acting out a Play Station game. He may be spinning his pencil around an imaginary object. He does it both at church and at home.

He has been complaining of his teeth not working right. They hurt. I believe he is getting his six-year molars in, causing the discomfort.

It was a full day. Andrew sat with us during the first fifteen minutes of the worship service and did well. He ate some Goldfish, tried to sing, and lowered his head during the prayer. He did just fine in his class: same room but different teachers.

Tonight, we went to the first part of the evening service where our family was introduced as a (somewhat) new family to the church. Andrew did not want to go back to the church. He wouldn't get out of the van. But once inside, he did fine. He sang quite loudly. He doesn't know the words but he would watch my mouth and try to match the shape and sound. When we finished singing, there was silence, which Andrew broke with a loud, "I'm real good at this!" People laughed; he was cute. I've been so proud of him.

August 20, 2003

Note from school:

Andrew continues to adapt well. He did especially well today. Mrs. Bland was absent, and he tolerated the change very well. Mrs. Bland reminded him several times this week that she would be gone. We read Social Stories regarding his teacher being out. He has grown a lot regarding this, and today couldn't have gone smoother.

August 29, 2003

Note from school:

Andrew had a hard time at lunch. He took his shirt partially off, pulled it over his head, and stuck his arms inside. He also pushed Tyler down in the lunch line.

September 5, 2003

Note from school:

Andrew began going to science lessons with Mrs. Bland this week. He has done very well! Who would have guessed? Next week, he is going to begin reading with me (Mrs. Brewer) instead of Mrs. Boren. This is because we feel that he is beyond her group. I am going to teach him the first-grade reading curriculum and follow what is being taught in the regular classroom. Hopefully, he will be able to progress into joining the regular classroom for reading one day. But for now, I think it may be better for him in small group.

September 23, 2003

I tried to help Andrew with his homework this afternoon. He told me, "Mommy, I know how to do it." So I left the room. He did it without my reading him the instructions, and he did it right! I'm so very excited to see his progress. It's wonderful!

September 27, 2003

So now, Andrew is seven. He is getting tall but is skinny as a beanpole. His face is changing. He's not a little boy any more. When did that happen? I must admit that I become torn with emotions around his birthday. I'm so pleased and thankful for the progress he has made and the potential for what lies ahead. But then I see what other children his age are doing and feel incredible sadness for how far he has to go to even "catch up."

It is amazing how every happy event has an underlying touch of sadness. It never goes away. It is constantly with me. Whenever tears of pride and joy prick my eyes, I know that a few of them are shed in sorrow.

October 1, 2003

Note from school:

I'm not sure what set Andrew off, but he yelled at two of the boys that he didn't like them. It was while we were circling up for morning meeting.

Andrew pushed two other boys on the playground very roughly. I gave him a time-out. When Ms. Andrea was bringing him back for science, he ran, slid on the floor, and wouldn't mind her.

Andrew wouldn't tell me what happened. I've noticed an increase in physical outbursts and feel it is frustration. I wonder if he is beginning to realize he is different. Yesterday, he said something funny but didn't intend to be funny. Jesse and his friends laughed. That made Andrew mad and he told them to stop laughing. When they didn't, he picked up a shoe and threw it at them. He also hit Jesse with a plastic bat.

He has become very rigid in how he thinks things should be at home and yells a lot. We're searching for answers. Perhaps he is getting ready for another breakthrough. He usually regresses right before he surges forward. I hope so.

October 2, 2003

Note from school:

Andrew was very frustrated today. He did okay this morning, but after lunch, he was pushing children and yelling at me. I put him in a time-out chair and when he got quiet, I said he could go back to his seat. He yelled that he didn't want to. I let him stay until he started yelling at me again. At the moment, he is yelling at me and saying, "You're making me look bad." I calmly said he could come to his seat, but he refused and continued to yell. Now, he is quiet. I told him if he continued to yell, I would take him to Mrs. Brewer.

He has changed in the past few weeks. I was thinking about his change of behavior and wonder if it is connected to him not bringing his blanket to school any more.

October 24, 2003

Note from school:

Andrew had a "G" in conduct for hitting a child with his lunch pail.

An Updated Diagnosis: Asperger Syndrome

❖

(October 2003 – July 2004)

October 30, 2003

Today, we took Andrew to a psychiatrist, Dr. Woods, to have him re-evaluated. It has been three years since we were told he has ASD. We haven't had any professional support outside of the school system since he started kindergarten.

Dr. Woods believes Andrew has Asperger's. I was, and am, shocked. I had always dismissed Asperger's because of Andrew's limited language. Now, it seems that isn't an issue. Andrew has language. I have the book *Asperger's Syndrome* by Tony Attwood. Maybe I'll figure out how this can be. I believe Dr. Woods. I just don't understand it.

I feel sad, although I'm not sure why. Maybe it was answering all the questions (95% of the time, the answer was "yes") that reminded me of Andrew's differences. Or maybe I was hoping Dr. Woods would say, "Wow, you know, it won't be long and Andrew won't even fit the autistic description." Whatever the reason, I feel sad. Yet, I can't stay here long. I need to accept this and move on to "so where do we go from here?"

November 8, 2003

If tomorrow never comes, and even if it does, I love you, Andrew. I am proud of you, too. You are smart and loving and can do so many things right. You are my sweet boy, and you always will be.

Christmas 2003

Andrew is seven years, three months old. He is 4'2" and weighs just 53 pounds. For the past eight months or so, he has been obsessed with baseball. He plays it inside and outside, on the computer, and even pretends objects are a baseball and bat. His favorite gifts this year all have to do with baseball. He also likes to play nerf basketball in the living room with Daddy. He is making his own jelly sandwiches, which he eats for almost every meal. He usually likes school.

January 5, 2004

Happy New Year! Andrew did far better this holiday season than he has the previous two. He still had issues but they weren't as severe as before. I'm curious to see how long it takes him to get back into his school routine. Not long, I should think.

January 6, 2004

Note from school:

Andrew had a good day yesterday. He seemed to adjust back into his routine just fine. He is a bit more chatty than usual, but I'm hoping that will decrease. He is doing well.

January 20, 2004

Andrew had an eye appointment. His right eye doesn't track as quickly as his left when following an object. Right now, we're in the "let's just watch it" stage, but we may be looking at strabismus surgery again somewhere down the road.

His big thing now is making books. He uses a lot of paper to "write" stories. He just can't grasp the concept of putting a space between the words, which makes it very difficult to read. He had a great report card, so he is keeping up academically with his peers.

February 3, 2004

Note from school:

Andrew had a meltdown today and would not work for me during reading. He did great during language, but at the beginning of reading, he began playing with his pencil. I told him to put it away, and he did. However, he kept reaching for it while we were reading. After I had told him three times to leave it alone, he went for it again. He went to time-out. When he returned, he cried and refused to work, no matter how hard I tried to redirect him. When his time in my classroom was over, he apologized.

February 4, 2004

Note from school:

Andrew gets very annoyed when "people are talking." I have noticed that he will smack the person's mouth who is sitting next to him. I'm trying to encourage him to use his words and not his hand. I have written a Social Story for this. I can only hope it helps.

February 5, 2004

I've realized I haven't done much writing in recent months. I really haven't since October. Yesterday, I saw the doctor and was diagnosed with a mild depression. It makes sense given my symptoms. I've struggled with depression for as long as I can remember. It's just gotten worse lately. I'm a little embarrassed to be taking an antidepressant. It's the pride factor and my own stereotyped ideas about it, but I'm willing to do whatever I need to do to feel better.

February 10, 2004

Note from school:

Andrew had a very tough time this morning. When he came into my classroom, he noticed Mrs. Cuppett [whom he knows from church] was subbing for Ms. Robin. I think this confused him. He became very upset with me and repeated, "I don't want to take people!" He cried and yelled at me for quite some time. His anger seemed to be directed only toward me. Anyway, I got him to work finally. I told him I would write a "happy" note if he worked for me. So, here is my "happy note."

February 11, 2004

Andrew has been a pill lately and easily tired. I'm not sure if he is getting sick or if he is just overly excited about being star of the week (similar reaction to his birthday). Donald and I are going out of town for a few days. I hope he'll be alright with Mema and Geda.

February 17, 2004

Well, my best friend Cara was right. The vacation didn't "cure" my depression. Yesterday was a rough day. It was a holiday so Andrew was home from school. Both boys were going at it. I lost it several times over simple irritants. I get so overwhelmed that it scares me. I hope this medicine helps soon. Perhaps Andrew is acting out in reaction to my problems?

February 19, 2004

Andrew has been pulling a lot of cards lately. He got an "N" in music on Tuesday because he pushed one boy down on purpose. He pulled a "G" in the classroom because he kept dropping his art box in the hall on purpose and laughing about it. I guess it made a great noise to him. He isn't cooperating with writing assignments. What's going on with this kid? Could I be affecting him this much?

March 11, 2004

Note from school:

Andrew has been asking for warnings and then asking to pull cards. His behavior has not warranted those actions. Today, it seemed he disobeyed on purpose so he could pull cards. At recess, he refused to come in when we lined up. Then, he just started yelling that he "didn't need to go" when we were in the hall. He wouldn't get in line. There were many tears at his desk with his blanket over his head.

March 22, 2004

I'm crazy. I have to be. I'm seriously considering home schooling Andrew, starting next year. Crazy, isn't it? Yet, I've always known I would be bringing him home eventually. Now, some friends are considering it for their kids so we've been talking about it. I find myself giving them all the right reasons and the advantages, and I wonder why I'm not applying them to Andrew. It seems right, but I wonder if I can.

March 23, 2004

Note from school:

Andrew got an "S" in music today because he would not follow directions. I witnessed about five minutes of that last part of the class period. The music teacher played a section of music and said the children could move any way they wanted but their hands and feet or knees were "stuck" to the floor. Andrew just ran around grabbing children. Apparently, he did that most of the class.

March 30, 2004

Andrew still hasn't come out of the "tough place" that he has been in for weeks. We are continuing to discuss home schooling him next year. It would be so easy to just get him off my hands for a while by sending him to school, but the behaviors he is displaying are a good cause

to home school him. It will be interesting. We only have a few weeks
to decide. The school will begin to implement the plan to adjust him
to second grade in mid-April. There is no reason to do that if he isn't
coming back. If we allowed it, and then pulled him, it may make the
adjustment that much harder.

We have decided to try Andrew on the medication Celexa for
obsessive-compulsive behavior, as Dr. Woods has suggested. We'll see
him on the 17th to get the prescription. Andrew has been obsessing an
incredible amount lately. It's worse than I've ever seen it.

[Author's note: Obsessive-compulsive disorder (OCD) is a brain disorder in which the brain gets stuck on a particular thought or urge and
can't let go. This disorder causes problems in information processing.
For more information, visit www.ocfoundation.org]

March 31, 2004

Note from school:

*Andrew was squeezing and trying to pick up children on the carpet. When
I told him to come and sit down, he started yelling and talking back to me. He
pushed my hands when I was reaching for his notebook to write you a note. He
is now screaming at me because I changed his card to an "S." He says, "I'll
never be in your class any more."*

I wish I knew how to help Mrs. Bland. Andrew yells at me all the
time. Nothing I do or say is right. We've had periods like this before
that have lasted up to two months. I wonder if he's getting ready for
another growth spurt. The other reason may be Tyler's birthday. He
has been obsessing over it for the past ten days. He talks about it all
the time, wanting to get him a lot of presents. I'll be ready to check
myself into the room with the padded walls if I hear about Tyler's
birthday one more time. It is today, so maybe we can get past this.

April 10, 2004

Andrew has been acting out a lot: screaming, yelling, kicking, pushing,
hitting. It was very embarrassing when he had a temper tantrum at
Jesse's baseball practice on Friday. He was yelling at me, "I don't want
to die!" He was quoting a movie. I told him repeatedly that he wasn't
going to die. I mumbled under my breath, "At least not yet." Another
mother heard me and started giggling. That eased my tension a little.

April 12, 2004

It looks like we will be home schooling both boys next fall. I can't say I'm excited yet. I'm still taking it all in. I feel like it's the right thing to do. Yesterday, I met with Mrs. Brewer and told her we would probably bring Andrew home. It was so hard to get the words out. I left with a heavy pit in my stomach, even though she was very gracious. I called Donald and he helped relieve the oppression that had weighed me down.

This is the right thing, he says. He had a peace about it, and he plans to be more involved than he currently is. So, why is this so difficult for me? I guess it's because it is a life-changing decision. It will change all of our lives. That scares me because I know I can't do it on my own. I have a tendency to run off on my own, without God, and that would be disastrous. Who do I think has brought me this far? It hasn't only been my own strength.

[Author's note: For anyone considering home schooling their special needs child, I highly recommend the book *Home Schooling Children with Special Needs* by Sharon C. Hensley.]

April 15, 2004

Note from school:

Andrew had an episode today where he was yelling at Mrs. Bland and not complying. He was saying that he was going to "kill" her. He was sent to the office and I (Mrs. Brewer) was called down. When I got there, Andrew was on the floor laughing and refusing to do what he was asked. After five minutes, I told him he had to come to my room. He did but did not want me to talk to him about how he had hurt Mrs. Bland's feelings. He said he was "certainly not going to apologize."

Once I got him to the room, I told him that he cannot treat his teachers that way. When he does, he can't be in their classrooms because their feelings have been hurt. Therefore, he needs to stay in my room until he is ready to apologize. When he realized he was missing recess and wasn't going to be able to play with his friends, he began to cry.

He cried for a while and decided to apologize. When he did, he was so sweet. He told Mrs. Bland he was sorry and he would never do it again. He said he couldn't help his tears. It was a sweet moment. Anyway, I wanted to let you know he had a tough afternoon.

The "I'm going to kill you" is a quote from *Charlotte's Web*. Needless to say, the movie was immediately taken away.

April 17, 2004

Dr. Woods told us that Asperger kids don't show the sign of Asperger's when they are by themselves. It's only when they have to interact with others. That's pretty funny, but it's true. We start Andrew on the Celexa medication tonight.

April 28, 2004

Note from school:

Andrew was licking Tyler at lunch and wouldn't stop when Tyler asked him to. They can't sit together at lunch for a while. Andrew says I yelled at him about the paper he uses. I just get louder than he does when he is talking back to me. He was very talkative and uncooperative in science so I let him go to the carpet.

May 7, 2004

Note from school:

Andrew is yelling at me because I made him sit down. He was spinning around the room and hitting children with his arms as he spun. He has calmed down and has stopped yelling. "Mrs. Bland, you didn't win. Here is your bad note!" He wanted me to know I was bad.

May 11, 2004

Wow, did we get some great news from the school. We had the IEP meeting for Andrew, even though the school knows we are going to keep him home. It enabled us to get a clear picture of where Andrew is in relation to the goals they had set for him. Mrs. Brewer did a series of grade placement tests with Andrew. These are fantastic.

> Word recognition – 2.7 grade
> Oral reading – 3.5 grade
> Basic sight vocabulary – read 399 out of 400 words
> Number words – read 36 out of 42 words
> Spelling – 3.5 grade
> Math – 2.0 grade (hasn't been allowed to work ahead)
> Reading vocabulary comprehension – 3.0 grade
> Reading comprehension – 3.0 grade

Not bad for a kid they warned us might have difficulty learning to read. And the school was very gracious in letting us know that if we decided to place Andrew back in the school, they would more than welcome him. His new IEP will stay valid until this time next year, just in case. We learned a lot about where his teachers and therapists think he is and what they feel are the most important things to work on.

May 14, 2004

Note from school:

Andrew had a tough afternoon. He and another boy "fought" going to math with Ms. Andrea. He cried and cried. He calmed down when inside recess came. He said he was sad because he wasn't being good.

May 26, 2004

Andrew is out of school tomorrow. He is so excited. While it will be nice to not have to be so concerned about getting him ready for school in the morning, I can't help but feel a little sad and nervous. We are turning a corner in our family life. By home schooling both boys, there is no "holding on until August." It's just, "here we go."

I'm nervous about how Andrew will do being home. How long will it take for him to adjust to doing school here? I've got what looks like a great book, *Social Skills Training*, specifically for Aspies. (That is a nickname for people with Asperger Syndrome.) I hope it helps. The hard part is deciding which skill to work on first. There are so many.

Jesse is actually excited about Andrew being home schooled with him. I wasn't sure how he would react, but he "voted" for it. I'm sure Andrew will get on his nerves at times, but fortunately, the house is big enough for them to have their own space when needed.

Andrew's been on the medicine for almost six weeks now. He's up to 3 ml a night. I can't see any improvement. He seems as obsessive as ever.

May 29, 2004

I don't know if I'm more angry or sad. Everything has to be on Andrew's terms. He dictates what he will eat, where he will sit, when I can go places. He gets to decide if I can tickle him or hug him. Sometimes I want to reach out and tickle him just because. He gets mad, and then I get mad.

It's a carry-over from yesterday. It has to be, or else I wouldn't be this close to tears. It was our first day home from school. It felt more like a Saturday than a Friday. I guess that's why I totally forgot about our appointment with Dr. Woods at 4:15 p.m. That is, until I glanced at the clock right at 4:15 and the light bulb went off in my head. I called the office and he was waiting on us. I have had to wait every single time we've been there. This was the one day he was on schedule.

We only live three minutes from the office, so it wouldn't have been so bad if Andrew would have cooperated. But no – the yelling began and he wouldn't get his shoes on or get in the van. I threw his shoes in the van, grabbed him, and "helped" him in. I couldn't afford the $50 fee for not showing up. Otherwise, I wouldn't have bothered. Bribery didn't work, Andrew was too far gone into his tantrum. So was I for that matter. It was the final straw that broke my grip on reality.

When we got to the office, Andrew wouldn't get out of the van and I couldn't reach him. It was humiliating to talk to Dr. Woods through the receptionist window in front of so many people while trying to keep an eye out their door to see my van. I busted my rear to get there, and there was no way to keep the appointment. I was mad at Dr. Woods for not coming out to the van, but now that I've calmed down, I see it was a stupid request. I just couldn't think straight at the time. He gave me the prescription I needed, and I ran out in tears. I have to call to reschedule; it'll take a month to get in.

I'm mad at myself for forgetting, although I'm not convinced it would have made a difference. Andrew had told me that morning that he wasn't going. I'm mad at Andrew that he is so disruptive and self-ish. Okay, the word is "egocentric," but it sure comes off as selfishness.

I've read in books, and people have said, that I can't let Andrew get away with normal kid behaviors. He has to learn to give in to cir-cumstances. But how? How do I know which behaviors are the As-perger's and which behaviors are being a seven-year-old? And how do I get him to learn? I get so tired of having my day revolve around him and his routines. This hasn't been a good way to kick off the summer.

June 3, 2004

It's a good day. The boys are playing well. The key is my consistency. Each day has to have the same rules, the same flexible schedule. An-drew still isn't happy with some of my "no's" but he is getting a little better at accepting them. I just have to stay calm.

June 10, 2004

We went to the zoo today: Mom, Jesse, my sister Yana, Andrew, and I. It was supposed to be something fun to do while they were in town visiting. Andrew was in an irritable mood and didn't really want to go, so he complained a lot. He only wanted to go to the playground. After a while, I took him there while the others saw more animals. It wasn't long before Andrew decided he was ready to go home. I told him we couldn't yet. He got mad and yelled, "I'm going home!" Then, he started to walk off. I watched him. I expected him to get to the edge of the playground and turn around to look at me. That's what he's always done before in similar situations. But he didn't this time. He just kept walking at a regular pace and didn't look back. I had to leave my things and run after him.

It was scary. I am so surprised that he would do that. I don't know if it was the disruption of everyone being here or the heat/humidity or what, but he has struggled the past couple of days.

June 15, 2004

Boy, has Andrew been a pill these past few days. He's had several screaming, door-slamming meltdowns. I haven't stuck to a schedule. Perhaps that's it, or could it be the medicine? We are up to 4 ml a night. I wonder if we are seeing a side effect.

I think the medicine might be helping. He doesn't pick at his fingers as much. He still talks to the Play Station and computer, but it doesn't seem to be as intense. I pray it is helping.

June 17, 2004

I think raising Andrew will only get harder as time goes by. Andrew himself is delightful most of the time. He makes me smile. But, oh, it hurts to watch him around other kids.

Like today. He is taking swimming lessons with three other kids in a private, backyard pool. Mr. Dennis is great and has over 25 years' experience dealing with kids with special needs, including autism. Andrew is doing very well considering he won't put his head under water. When it isn't his turn, he talks or sings to himself or just stares while picking his fingers. The other kids look at him, then look at each other and giggle. Seeing Andrew through their eyes, who can blame them? He's a strange boy who talks funny and doesn't always act "normal." But it hurts.

I want to snatch him up and run away from the stares and laughter. I don't want to deal with the unspoken awkwardness of the other parents who don't know what to say and are too polite to ask, "What's wrong with him, anyway?" I had to fight back some tears. How much longer until Andrew notices that he is different? What then?

I can't run away. If I give in now, he will lose out on so much. Yet, it is so hard to stay; hard to make myself let him do these things. It will get harder the older he gets. The gulf between his development and that of other kids his age widens each year. Andrew may not notice but the kids do – and I do, too, and it hurts.

June 22, 2004

Where did I read it recently? When we face trouble, we often look at the past to see what we've done. It was that way for me with Andrew. When the ASD was becoming more obvious and we got the diagnosis, I thought I was being punished for something. I couldn't figure out what I had done that was so terrible that my son would suffer – that we would all suffer. But I'm not being punished. I need to look forward and not backward.

June 29, 2004

Donald is right. Tonight is not the time to make any decisions. It's been a long day. I've had a headache all day – woke up with one – and it hasn't let up. Stress. Andrew.

In some ways, it is easier having Andrew home all the time. We sleep later, which is definitely better for all of us. We rarely have any place we have to go, so I can be more flexible and plan errands for when he is in a cooperative mood.

Yet, that very flexibility may be causing some of the problems. I haven't set a schedule yet. I struggle, too. Andrew is so loud, and I get tired of telling him to quiet down. Plus, he has added a very annoying literary problem. He keeps adding a short "a" sound to the end of his phrases. "It's a ball-a." It's driving me nuts-a!

I've tried to do a little school work with him. Math is okay. Spelling is causing me headaches. He can spell the words, but he doesn't like the exercises that go with the words, such as definitions and syllables. He just guesses because he wants to go do something else. It is aggravating.

I guess I thought he would be doing better by now, because of his age. He's almost eight. He either doesn't know or doesn't care that he's different. I think the former. Some day, he will care and then perhaps he will let us help him rather than fighting us.

I took Andrew to Dr. Woods for a follow-up on his medicine. I was surprised. I thought we were at full strength at 5 ml a night. Apparently, we are just getting started. So, it's okay that we haven't noticed a big change. It may help yet. We will be going up to two teaspoons a night for a few months. So far, Andrew won't take any pills, even the chewable kind. But we need to do something because it is becoming unreasonable to continue the liquids. It tastes nasty. It's hard for him to get down that much liquid. I think we can grind the pills.

I was frustrated tonight and embarrassed at Andrew's loud voice and behavior at Jesse's ballgame. I am beginning to doubt that I can do this. Can I home school him? What have I gotten myself into?

June 30, 2004

I wasn't sure how I was going to sit here and journal without crying. I'm in the hallway at church, so I didn't want to cry. But then Mrs. Sheri sat down next to me and I couldn't help myself. She knew I was upset and her concern started the flood. Her youngest daughter has special needs, so she knows.

Andrew threw a fit about being here tonight. He was fine walking into the building but then started screaming. At one point, he tried to run away. When I went to catch him, he dodged me. So, I started to walk away and he practically tackled me from behind. Let's face it. I was embarrassed and angry. No, I was very embarrassed and very angry.

July 13, 2004

My friend JoAnn stopped by last night just to give me a hug. It was sweet and appreciated, especially since at that moment, I was embattled with a naked Andrew, who was refusing to take a bath. It was getting late. I know I'm supposed to stay calm, but it can be so hard. I picked him up and dumped him in the tub. What a night.

This Saturday, I'm going to speak to a class of teachers who are getting training in special education. They wanted someone who could share what a day in the life of a family with autism is like. I'm looking forward to it. I appreciate the opportunity to educate people about ASD and what it is really like. Donald and I have been reminiscing on Andrew memories – such bitter-sweet memories.

July 22, 2004

What a wonderful day for Andrew. He is growing up and becoming more and more independent. Today at Uncle Steve's pool, he swam from one side of the pool to the other all by himself, without touching, many times. He is so proud of himself, as he should be. He still won't put his head under water but surely that will come some day. I can't totally relax around the pool, but I do feel a little better about him.

Tonight, he showered and washed his hair all by himself. He did his chores (cat box and backyard) by himself. It is exciting to see the independence in positive ways. I still have to closely monitor the "less positive" aspects such as going to someone's house without telling me and getting snacks all day long without asking. But, he is coming along!

It's amazing how one good day can erase several bad days. Those good days are my hope. They represent Andrew's potential. If I can stay calm and work him through the difficult days, then just maybe we'll see a lot more good days.

Ending One Chapter, Starting Another: Parting Thoughts

❖

(July 31, 2004)

July 31, 2004

I feel like a chapter of our lives is closing. In two days, we will begin a new school year. Andrew is in second grade and Jesse is in fifth. I stopped trying to do any type of school work with Andrew. Instead, we have been talking about the first day of school and how much fun it will be. He is getting very excited. I fully expect some kind of meltdown in the middle of the week when the newness wears off. But overall, I feel much more confident and at peace. I'm ready. I just know it will be a good year.

I am remembering all the reasons we have for keeping Andrew at home. Last year, he would do well at school (most of the time) for more than seven hours. Then, he would come home and fall apart. He didn't want anything more to do with school, especially homework. School was school and home was home, and the two should not mix! He would be tired of being cooperative and was more likely to yell, be disrespectful and disobedient. It was hard. I would hear about this terrific kid. *I* wanted to see that terrific kid. I miss that.

When Andrew would bring papers home, I was never sure how much he did on his own and how much help he had needed. I'm uncertain of what he really knows. It amazes me that he can read aloud quite well, yet not understand what he is reading. I guess it's like me reading Spanish. I can pronounce the words, but I can't tell you what they mean.

The school also had to let him do busywork to keep him from distracting the other kids. He must have gone through several reams of paper throughout the year with the number of "books" he made and drawings he brought home. I think we can accomplish at least as much in less time. He seems to learn best when working one-on-one with someone. There's no reason why that "someone" can't be me. Having said that, I recognize that home schooling is not for everyone. Each family has to decide what is best for them.

There are times when Jesse can get Andrew to do things I can't. I may be too quick to excuse Andrew or to help him. Jesse pushes him to do things neither one of us thought he was capable of. I've been pleased that they are getting along better. They still fight, but they usually make up in a short time. That is being typical siblings. I think Jesse is finally seeing that Andrew has a lot to teach him about compassion, patience, and perseverance.

I've been taking the boys to church on Wednesday nights. There are a lot of kids there. It has been a test for us to see how well Andrew can handle the large number of people and the loud noises. He can still get overstimulated and we watch that carefully. But overall, he has done remarkably well. I have been very pleased. As little as six months ago, he would not have been able to handle that kind of setting.

He is starting soccer practice soon. He loves the Teenage Mutant Ninja Turtles. It is good to finally see him interested in something besides baseball. He also likes to race: toy cars, bikes, on the Play Station. He eats constantly and is still stuck on jelly sandwiches, applesauce, and vanilla ice cream. He doesn't have any "friends" in the sense of a close buddy, but there are children who will tolerate his behavior and play with him.

When I watch Andrew today, I'm in awe. He barely resembles the four-year-old child we had tested. He talks non-stop and can express himself fairly well. He makes eye contact and loves to give hugs. He tolerates people touching him for short periods of time. He is learning how to lower his voice when reminded so he isn't loud all the time.

Andrew continues to become more and more aware that he is different from the other kids. He is noticing that when the kids laugh, they are laughing at him. He didn't pay attention to that before. It makes him angry and hurt. He yells at them to stop laughing and may try to hit them. Usually, he comes and buries himself in my lap and sobs. I've talked with some of the kids. We passed a booklet on autism around the neighborhood and asked parents to read it to their kids. Still, sometimes Andrew says things that are really funny. It's hard not to laugh. The only problem is, he doesn't mean to be funny so he gets angry when we laugh. I give him credit, though. He keeps going out there, trying to make friends. I'm proud of him, even when it hurts my heart.

Andrew still gets easily overwhelmed. He continues to be egocentric, believing the world revolves around him and his needs. He is aggressive, loud, and disrespectful one moment and then sweet, contrite, and loving the next. He keeps us on a perpetual roller-coaster ride of uncertainty.

When I look back at where we have come from, it has been quite a journey. We've tried new things, met many wonderful people, and learned things we never dreamed. Andrew sees the world differently than the rest of us. Sometimes, I get a glimpse into the world he sees, and it is a fascinating, often scary, place. At other times, I just shake my head and wonder what color the sky is in his world. I'm thankful for each lesson and each bend in the road.

When I look at Andrew's future, I have great hope. He is intelligent, even when he can't express it. He is outgoing and aware of what's going on around him. He acknowledges and talks to strangers, introducing himself and asking for their name. We have a tremendous support system of family, friends, professionals, and church family. God has truly blessed us.

I don't know what the future will bring, so it can also be a bit scary. We still go through times when we wonder if where we are now is as good as it is going to get. Andrew will get stuck for weeks on end without any visible progress. Sometimes, he even regresses. Usually, it comes before some kind of growth spurt: physical, emotional, or intellectual. I have to remind myself that Andrew has had many setbacks before. It doesn't mean we've done something wrong or that he has already reached his potential. It is just part of the ASD dance of taking a step backward before taking those important steps forward. It's a good thing I love to dance.

He is my Andrew. He is my sweet boy. He always will be.

Resources

❖

The following is not an exhaustive list but reflects resources I have found helpful in my own search for information.

Websites

www.americanequestrian.com/hippotherapy.htm
American Hippotherapy Association: provides information on using horses as therapy.

www.aspergers.com
Asperger's disorder home page: answers questions and gives resource links.

www.autism-pdd.net
A guide to the key issues associated with autism spectrum disorders.

www.autism-resources.com
Autism Resources: offers information and links regarding autism and Asperger Syndrome.

www.autism-society.org
Autism Society of America: the leading source of information, research, and references on autism.

www.childrensdisabilities.info
Children's Disabilities Information: empowers parents of children with special needs.

www.difflearn.com
Different Roads to Learning: dedicated to providing ASD resources.

www.ed.gov/parents/needs/speced/iepguide
A government website to assist educators, parents, and educational agencies in implementing the Individuals with Disabilities Education Act (IDEA) and Individualized Education Programs (IEPs).

www.eplibrary.com
The Exceptional Parent: a bookstore with resources related to kids with special needs.

www.asperger.net
The Autism Asperger Publishing Company: a leading source of information on autism and Asperger Syndrome.

www.gfcfdiet.com
Offers resources for gluten-free, casein-free diet.

www.kidshealth.org
Provides medical information from the Nemours Foundation. Information is available for parents, kids, and teens.

www.kirkmanlabs.com
Manufacturer of products, including vitamin and dietary supplements, such as Super Nu-Thera vitamins.

www.linguisystems.com
Offers resources for speech and language, learning disabilities, and reading.

www.mayoclinic.com
Provides medical information from the Mayo Clinic.

www.newdiets.com
Features gluten-free, casein-free recipes.

www.nightterrors.org
Night Terror Resource Center: gives information on night terrors.

www.ocfoundation.org
Obsessive-Compulsive Foundation: gives information about obsessive-compulsive disorders.

www.parent-magic.com
ParentMagic, Inc.: dedicated to helping parents build strong, positive relationships with their children. Best known for the parenting program, 1-2-3 Magic.

www.preemiemum.com/touchpressure_technique_.htm
Touch-Pressure Technique: provides information about brush therapy.

www.sensoryresources.com
Resources for raising children with sensory-motor, developmental, and social-emotional challenges.

www.sensorytools.net
Sensory integration tools and resources.

www.specialkidszone.com
Achievement products for children: offers hundreds of therapy, exercise and special education products.

www.superduperinc.com
Resources for speech-language therapists, special educators, preschool teachers, resource and reading teachers.

Suggested Reading

Anderson, E., & Emmons, P. (1996). *Unlocking the mysteries of sensory dysfunction: A resource for anyone who works with, or lives with, a child with sensory issues.* Arlington, TX: Future Horizons.

Attwood, T. (1998). *Asperger's Syndrome: A guide for parents and professionals.* London: Jessica Kingsley Publishers.

Baker, J. E. (2003). *Social skills training for children and adolescents with Asperger Syndrome and social-communication problems.* Shawnee Mission, KS: Autism Asperger Publishing Company.

Bashe, P. R., & Kirby, B. L. (2001). *The oasis guide to Asperger Syndrome: Advice, support, insights, and inspiration.* New York: Crown Publishing.

Brill, M. T. (1994). *Keys to parenting the child with autism.* New York: Barron's Educational Series, Inc.

Buron, K. D. (2006). *When my worries get too big!* Shawnee Mission, KS: Autism Asperger Publishing Company.

Buron, K. D., & Curtis, M. (2003). *The incredible 5-point scale: Assisting students with autism spectrum disorders in understanding social interactions and controlling their emotional responses.* Shawnee Mission, KS: Autism Asperger Publishing Company.

Cohen, J. (2002). *The Asperger parent: How to raise a child with Asperger Syndrome and maintain your sense of humor.* Shawnee Mission, KS: Autism Asperger Publishing Company.

Cohen, J. (2006). *Guns a'blazing: How parents of children on the autism spectrum and schools can work together – without a shot being fired.* Shawnee Mission, KS: Autism Asperger Publishing Company.

Elliott, L. B. (2002). *Embarrassed often, ashamed never: Quips and short stories from one family's ongoing adventure with Asperger Syndrome and autism.* Shawnee, Mission, KS: Autism Asperger Publishing Company.

Ernsperger, L., & Stegen-Hanson, T. (2004). *Just take a bite: Easy, effective answers to food aversions and eating challenges!* Arlington, TX: Future Horizons.

Gagnon, E. (2001). *Power cards: Using special interests to motivate children and youth with Asperger Syndrome and autism.* Shawnee Mission, KS: Autism Asperger Publishing Company.

Grandin, T. (1995). *Thinking in pictures: And other reports from my life with autism.* New York: Vintage Books.

Gray, C. (2000). *The new social stories book.* Arlington, TX: Future Horizons.

Hamilton, L. M. (2000). *Facing autism: Giving parents reasons for hope and guidance for help.* Colorado Springs, CO: WaterBrook Press.

Hensley, S. C. (1995). *Home schooling children with special needs: Turning challenges into opportunities!* Gresham, OR: Noble Publishing Associates.

Herzog, J. (1994). *Learning in spite of labels: Practical teaching tips and a Christian perspective of education.* Lebanon, TN: Greenleaf Press.

Hodgdon, L. A. (1999). *Solving behavior problems in autism: Improving communication with visual strategies.* Troy, MI: Quirk Roberts Publishing.

Jackson, L. (2002). *Freaks, geeks, and Asperger Syndrome: A user guide to adolescence.* London: Jessica Kingsley Publishers.

Jaffe, A. N., & Gardner, L. (2006). *My book full of feelings: How to control and react to the size of your emotions.* Shawnee Mission, KS: Autism Asperger Publishing Company.

Kranowitz, C. S. (1998). *The out-of-sync child: Recognizing and coping with sensory integration dysfunction.* New York: Berkley Publishing Group.

Lentz, K. (2004). *Hopes and dreams: An IEP guide for parents of children with autism spectrum disorders.* Shawnee Mission, KS: Autism Asperger Publishing Company.

Lewis, L. (1998). *Special diets for special kids: Understanding and implementing special diets to aid in the treatment of autism and related developmental disorders.* Arlington, TX: Future Horizons.

Lieberman, L. A. (2005). *A "stranger" among us: Hiring in-home support for a child with autism spectrum disorders or other neurological differences.* Shawnee Mission, KS: Autism Asperger Publishing Company.

Manasco, H. (2006). *The way to a: Empowering children with autism spectrum and other neurological disorders to monitor and replace aggression and tantrum behavior.* Shawnee Mission, KS: Autism Asperger Publishing Company.

Myles, B. S. (2006). *The hidden curriculum: One-a-day calendar: Items for understanding unstated rules in social situations.* Shawnee Mission, KS: Autism Asperger Publishing Company.

Myles, B. S., Cook, K. T., Miller, N. E., Rinner, L., & Robbins, L. A. (2000). *Asperger Syndrome and sensory issues: Practical solutions for making sense of the world.* Shawnee Mission, KS: Autism Asperger Publishing Company.

Myles, B. S., & Southwick, J. (2005). *Asperger Syndrome and difficult moments: Practical solutions for tantrums, rage, and meltdowns.* Shawnee Mission, KS: Autism Asperger Publishing Company.

Myles, B. S., Trautman, K. L., & Schelvan, R. L. (2004). *The hidden curriculum: Practical solutions for understanding unstated rules in social situations.* Shawnee Mission, KS: Autism Asperger Publishing Company.

Myles, H. M. (2005). *Practical solutions to everyday challenges for children with Asperger Syndrome.* Shawnee Mission, KS: Autism Asperger Publishing Company.

Naseef, R. A. (2001). *Special children, challenged parents: The struggles and rewards of raising a child with a disability.* Baltimore: Paul H. Brookes Publishing Company.

Sakai, K. (2005). *Finding our way: Practical solutions for creating a supporting home and community for the Asperger Syndrome family.* Shawnee Mission, KS: Autism Asperger Publishing Company.

Savner, J. L., & Myles, B. S. (2000). *Making visuals work in the home and community: Strategies for individuals with autism and Asperger Syndrome.* Shawnee Mission, KS: Autism Asperger Publishing Company.

Summers, L. (2005). *Autism is not a life sentence. How one family took on autism and won!* Shawnee Mission, KS: Autism Asperger Publishing Company.

Tobias, C. U. (1994). *The way they learn: How to discover and teach to your child's strengths.* Wheaton: IL: Tyndale House Publishers, Inc.

Wheeler, M. (1998). *Toilet training for individuals with autism & related disorders.* Arlington, TX: Future Horizons Inc.

Glossary

❖

Asperger Syndrome – a disorder on the autism spectrum marked by impaired social skills as well as repetitive and stereotypical behaviors. It is also referred to as high-functioning autism. Generally, there is no significant delay in language or self-help skills.

Autism – sometimes called "classic" autism. It is a disorder on the autism spectrum in which a child is markedly impaired in the use of language, reaction to stimuli, interpretation of the world, and the formation of relationships.

Autism Spectrum Disorder – a term that encompasses five neurological disorders impacting the normal development of the brain in the areas of social interaction and communication skills. There is no test for ASD. Diagnosis is made taking into account family history, medical issues, and observations.

Brush Therapy – a therapy used to decrease tactile defensiveness. It involves "brushing" certain parts of the body at regular intervals. It is to be initiated and monitored by an occupational or physical therapist.

Echolalia – involuntary repetition of words or phrases either just spoken by others or delayed for days, weeks, or months.

Electroencephalogram (EEG) – a record of the electrical impulse activity in the brain.

Expressive Language – words used to convey thoughts, ideas, or needs.

Fine-Motor Skills – the ability to use the small muscles in the hands, fingers, face and tongue to make precise, detailed movements. An example would be the ability to open/close a zipper or string beads.

Gross-Motor Skills – the ability to use large-muscle groups such as the legs, arms, and stomach. An example would be the ability to ride a bicycle.

Hippotherapy – treatment by trained therapists who use the multidimensional movement of a horse as a tool to address functional limitations and disabilities. The Greek word "hippos" means horse.

Inclusion – service delivery option in schools where children with disabilities are placed with typically developing children.

Individuals with Disabilities Education Act (IDEA) – law that ensures all children with disabilities receive a free, appropriate public education in the least restrictive environment while meeting the child's individual needs.

Individualized Education Program (IEP) – an education plan tailored to the individual needs of the child that includes goals, objectives, and evaluation standards.

Night Terrors – a sudden awakening from sleep in a condition of extreme fear that is not associated with a dream or nightmare.

Obsessive-Compulsive Disorder (OCD) – a condition marked by obsessive thoughts combined with repetitive actions. An example is the child who needs things in a certain order (obsession) and, therefore, always lines up or straightens objects (compulsive).

Occupational Therapist (OT) – a therapist who specializes in improving the development of fine-motor skills and may address sensory integration needs.

Pervasive Developmental Disorder-Not Otherwise Specified (PDD-NOS) – a diagnosis on the autism spectrum that is used for children who do not fully meet the criteria for one of the other disorders on the spectrum.

Physical Therapist (PT) – a therapist who specializes in improving the development of both gross- and fine-motor skills and may address sensory integration needs.

Proprioceptive Sense – refers to the muscles, joints, and tendons that provide a person with a subconscious awareness of body position or where one's body is in space.

Receptive Language – the ability to understand words, gestures, and written communication.

Sensory Integration – the ability to take in information through the senses, to put it together with prior experiences and knowledge, and to give an appropriate response.

Speech Language Therapist (SL) – a therapist who works to improve speech, language, and communication skills.

Tactile Sense – the system of nerves under the skin that sends information to the brain; includes taste, texture, pain, pressure, and temperature.

Vestibular Sense – the sensory system in the inner ear that detects movement and changes in the position of the head. Dysfunction in this area may be manifested by either a fear of ordinary movement activities (e.g., slides or swings) or an intense desire to stimulate the vestibular sense (e.g., excessive spinning or jumping).

AAPC Practical Solutions Series –
A Must for Parents and Educators

This best-selling series offers sound, practical information and advice on everyday challenges related to autism spectrum disorders. From sensory issues to social situations, education and behavior, there's a title to fit the need.

2006 ASA LITERARY AWARD WINNER!
Finding Our Way: Practical Solutions for Creating a Supportive Home and Community for the Asperger Syndrome Family
Kristi Sakai

Asperger Syndrome and Sensory Issues: Practical Solutions for Making Sense of the World
Brenda Smith Myles, Katherine Tapscott Cook, Nancy E. Miller, Louann Rinner, and Lisa A. Robbins

Asperger Syndrome and the Elementary School Experience: Practical Solutions for Academic & Social Difficulties
Susan Thompson Moore

Perfect Targets: Asperger Syndrome and Bullying; Practical Solutions for Surviving the Social World
Rebekah Heinrichs

Asperger Syndrome and Difficult Moments: Practical Solutions for Tantrums, Rage, and Meltdowns (Revised and Expanded Edition)
Brenda Smith Myles and Jack Southwick

Asperger Syndrome and Adolescence: Practical Solutions for School Success
Brenda Smith Myles, Ph.D., and Diane Adreon

The Hidden Curriculum: Practical Solutions for Understanding Unstated Rules in Social Situations
Brenda Smith Myles, Melissa L. Trautman, and Ronda L. Schelvan

Practical Solutions to Everyday Challenges for Children with Asperger Syndrome
Haley Morgan Myles